Pearl Harbor -

A Day of Infamy

Robert J Mueller

A Fields of War Visitor's Guide to Historic Sites

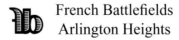 French Battlefields
Arlington Heights

French Battlefields
PO Box 4808
Buffalo Grove, Illinois 60089-4808
Email: contact@frenchbattlefields.com
Web address: http://www.frenchbattlefields.com

Cover photographs:
Color: Entrance gate to the National Cemetery of the Pacific
Timeline: The USS *Arizona* explodes after a Japanese bomb penetrates the deck and detonates the forward
powder magazine. (left). NARA
A B-17C stands on Hickam Field with its tail section burned off by magnesium flares, (center). NARA
The moment the USS *Shaw* explodes as seen from across the harbor; note a gun turret of the USS
Pennsylvania is barely visible on the right side of the photograph, (right). NARA

Abbreviations used for photographs:
NARA: National Archives and Records Administration, College Park, Maryland
NHHC: United States Navy Naval History and Heritage Command
USAF: United States Air Force
USN: United States Navy

Dedicated to:
Those who served

Introduction

Hawaii was a different place. Life proceeded at a slower and friendlier pace. Greetings and conversation were required ingredients to every interaction – even among strangers. Perhaps the relaxed life style, the ambience of Waikiki's beachfront hotels, and the pleasures of Honolulu's Hotel Street red-light district contributed to the military's unpreparedness of 1941.

Today, Hawaii retains much of that lifestyle despite Oahu traffic congestion and the smothering hordes of sun-loving tourists. Highways post lower speed limits than one might expect – what is the hurry? Even the most aggressive urban dweller requires only a few days to depressurize and accept slower, but friendlier restaurant service, 'Alohas' from everyone, and the soothing murmur of beachfront waves.

This pamphlet explores the major and minor locations of the Second World War on Oahu. Although other islands of the Hawaiian chain became involved in the war as training grounds or defensive installations after 7 December 1941, only Oahu was attacked on that date. Specific tour routes are not presented since visitors will map out sites that fit their interest and schedules.

The information contained herein is believed to be accurate at the time of printing, but museum hours are notoriously subject to change. If access to a certain site is of paramount importance, it is best to contact it in advance. American military cemeteries are handicap accessible, but their hours are restricted from 08:00 to 18:00. An American representative is always on duty to assist relatives to locate graves of family members.

Each year roadways are improved or re-routed and intersections reconstructed. Therefore, up-to-date road maps or GPS locators are a necessity. Geographic coordinates (latitude, longitude), which can be entered into GPS locators, are given for each location allowing visitors to select those sites of individual interest or to alter the order of visitation. For those unable or unwilling to provide their own transportation, tour companies offer a reasonable alternative and frequently provide the military sponsorship necessary to enter otherwise restricted areas.

The Path to War

Japan to the 1930s

Japan was opened to Western influence with the arrival of a squadron of the United States Navy commanded by Commodore Matthew Perry in 1853. At the time, the four main islands comprising Japan presented an area about the size of California. In the late 19th century, Japan gained control over Korea, Formosa, the southern tip of Manchuria, and the Liaotung (Liaodong) peninsula[1] through military adventurism. Rapid industrialization of the feudal empire resulted in internal political conflict, social injustice, bribery, and corruption. By the 1930s the island nation of 80 million people suffered wide-spread unemployment among urban dwellers and near starvation for the rural population. To many the antidote was nationalism and militarism.

The thinly-populated wilderness of Manchuria was seen as an opportunity to relieve homeland unemployment through sourcing badly needed raw materials. The vast territory had already been the scene of conflict between Chinese and Russian interests, which resulted in the area being loosely governed by a Chinese warlord. The Japanese Kwantung Army provided security to merchants and traders with its guardianship of Manchuria's rail network; however, rebel Kwantung Army officers desired complete control of Manchuria for Japan. On 18 September 1931 they manufactured an incident in Mukden by planting a dynamite charge under the tracks of the Japanese protected South Manchuria Railway. The explosion near a Chinese Army barracks provided the necessary excuse to occupy the city of Mukden. Despite direct orders from the Japanese Army General Staff, the Kwantung Army proceeded to sweep through the rest of Manchuria and established a puppet government over the renamed territory of Manchukuo.

Amid deepening economic depression, the power of right-wing militarists grew. In February 1936, a rebellion by 1,400 young radical officers and men led to the assassination of several advisors to the emperor. The rebellion rapidly dissipated, but it fermented a policy of permanent expansion of the Empire of Japan. The Army gained control over the appointment of the War Minister and eventually political control of the country.

The Marco Polo Bridge Incident

Western and Japanese troops had been stationed in the Chinese capital of Peking (Beijing) since the suppression of the Boxer Rebellion in 1900. The rise of Chinese nationalism under Dr Sun Yat-sen[2] was furthered by his successor Chiang Kai-shek. Eventually Chiang struck an accord with Mao Tse-tung, leader of the Chinese Communists, to drive the Japanese from North China.

On 7 July 1937, at an old stone bridge named by westerners after the famed Italian explorer Marco Polo, Chinese troops fired upon a Japanese Army unit undergoing a night training exercise. After a short exchange and a single Japanese casualty, the skirmish ended.

---

1 The Liaodong peninsula is in the northern part of the Yellow Sea. The mountainous area was the scene of major fighting during the Russo-Japanese War of 1904 – 1905.

2 We have retained the Chinese naming convention of surname first.

A second Japanese company rushed to the scene. As the Chinese and Japanese officers discussed re-establishing the local truce, a second volley of rifle fire struck the Japanese troops. Although controversy exists to this day as to who fired the second shots, they appear to have originated from Chinese Communist troops hoping to instigate warfare between the Japanese and Chiang Kai-shek's nationalist forces.

The incident was quickly resolved, but the expansionist elements of the Japanese Army General Staff argued that Chiang might retake Manchuria, threaten Japanese-occupied Korea, and lead to Soviet and Chinese Communist domination of Asia. On the night of 25 July 1937, fighting broke out near Langfang, a city on the rail line between Peking (Beijing) and Tientsin (Tianjin). The conflict escalated and a Japanese punitive expedition was launched. War had come to China.

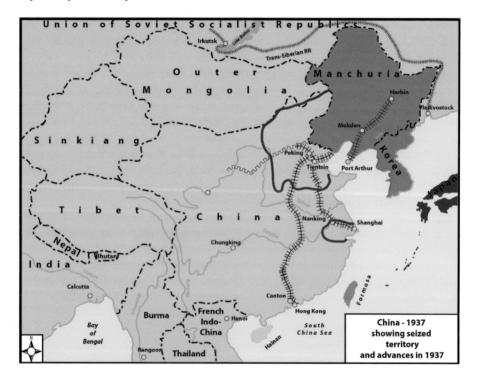

China - 1937 showing seized territory and advances in 1937

Western Involvement in Asia

Western governments condemned the Japanese actions. In October, United States President Franklin D Roosevelt spoke against the aggression equating the Japanese to the Nazis. The League of Nations censured Japan.[3] In mid-December Japanese airplanes bombed the US gunboat *Panay* on the Yangtze River as it evacuated American citizens from the then Chinese capital of Nanking (Nanjing). Roosevelt responded by proposing that Great Britain join America in a naval blockade of Japan. Prime Minister Neville Chamberlain refused. Instead Roosevelt accepted a formal

---

3   Japan had withdrawn from the League of Nations in 1933 after condemnation of its actions in Manchuria.

apology.

Later that month, Japanese Army forces entered Nanking. Army troops began an occupation that included looting, raping, and murdering the civilian population. The 'Rape of Nanking,' as the incident became known, continued for a month with as many as 300,000 civilians brutally slaughtered.

The Japanese Army continued to achieve victories on the field but condemnation from Western governments. For the Japanese, the Sino-Japanese War had evolved into a holy war to free Asia from colonial and communist forces. America denounced Japanese aggression while the Japanese compared their actions in China to the Monroe Doctrine and colonial powers. Why were British and Dutch occupations of India, Hong Kong, Singapore, and the East Indies acceptable, but Japanese conquest of China was a crime? Why, indeed?

The outbreak of the Second World War in Europe and the subsequent defeat of the Netherlands, Belgium, and France in the spring of 1940 by the Nazis struck the Japanese Army General Staff as an opportunity to secure the tin, tungsten, coal, and rice of Southeast Asia. On 27 September 1940, Japan signed the Tripartite Pact with Germany and Italy guaranteeing reciprocal defense if any signee were attacked. Roosevelt was convinced that the three 'gangster' nations had joined forces to conquer the world. The US retaliated by adding machine tools, iron, steel, copper, and bronze to the previously announced embargoes of high-grade scrap iron and aviation fuel.

The German invasion of the Soviet Union in June 1941 brought a conundrum to the Japanese government. Should it join its ally Germany and attack Soviet Siberia to the north? Or maintain its current focus on Southeast Asia? Either decision risked conflict with the United States. Despite the protests of the foreign minister, Japan targeted mineral-rich Indochina and oil-rich Dutch East Indies (Indonesia). On 24 July the German-puppet Vichy French government was informed that the Japanese Army would enter French Indochina. Two days later Roosevelt ordered all Japanese assets in America frozen. Britain and the Dutch government-in-exile quickly followed suit. The action embargoed all exports.

Feeling the pressure of shrinking oil reserves coupled with American demands for the withdrawal of Japanese troops from Indochina and all of China, Japanese Prime Minister and Army General Hideki Tojo established a 26 November deadline for concluding a peace agreement with the United States. Diplomatic bungling and mutual distrust coupled with Japanese intentions not to lose face derailed the negotiations over the issue of Japanese troop withdrawals.

Spy versus Spy

In 1940, Lieutenant Colonel William F Friedman, US Army Signal Corps, cracked the Japanese diplomatic code named PURPLE. The resulting decoded and translated material was called MAGIC. Throughout the months of negotiations between Secretary of State Cordell Hull and Japan's ambassador in Washington, Kichisaburo Nomura, American cryptologists read the ambassador's instructions received from Tokyo. Distribution of MAGIC was tightly controlled with only twelve high-level government officials receiving MAGIC messages.

On 27 March 1941, Takeo Yoshikawa, a trained intelligence agent, arrived in Oahu. Local geography greatly assisted his espionage efforts against Pearl Harbor. Moorings and sailings of American ships in the naval basin could easily be seen from the Aiea area hills to the east.

On 24 September, the Japanese Foreign Ministry sent exacting and detailed observation instructions that requested accurate models of Pearl Harbor, positions and armaments of American ships, sailing routines, disposition of aircraft, and timing and range of PBY flying boat reconnaissance missions. Heretofore, requests had been for general information regarding the Pacific Fleet. The unusual interest in Pearl Harbor caught the attention of Colonel Rufus Bratton, head of the Far East Section of Army Intelligence. The MAGIC source of the information restricted its distribution despite Bratton's belief that Hawaii was in eminent danger.

Negotiations with Japan stalled and on 27 November 1941, Secretary of War Henry Stimson sent a warning message of impending hostilities to the Philippines, the Panama Canal Department, the Western Defense Command (which had responsibility for Alaska), and the Hawaiian Department. It clearly stated that the message was to be considered a war warning. The message included instructions to prepare for War Plan 46. Also on 27 November, British observers reported a large Japanese expeditionary force steaming south from Shanghai.

On 3 December a MAGIC memorandum reported that the Japanese consulate in Honolulu was ordered to increase its reports on the location of American warships in Pearl Harbor. On 5 December, the wife of a local Japanese dentist held an extended telephone conversation with a Tokyo newspaper regarding planes, weather conditions, and local flowers. The call was intercepted and translated attracting the attention of the FBI, but local commanders remained skeptical. That same day, Yoshikawa performed his last scouting of the Pacific Fleet and forwarded the information by coded commercial telegraph.[4] Meanwhile, aides burned wheel borrows full of documents in the consulate courtyard.

American troops on Oahu received their normal peacetime Saturday night liberty.

Japanese Attack Plan

Admiral Isoroku Yamamoto[5] was a strong proponent of naval aviation, but a publically outspoken opponent of Japan going to war against the United States. So great were the threats of his assassination by political opponents that he was placed on sea duty as Commander in Chief of the Japanese Combined Fleet for his own protection. Nevertheless, the concept of an air attack by carrier based planes developed in Yamamoto's mind after he witnessed Japanese fleet maneuvers in 1940. By February 1941, Yamamoto's outline for a daring preemptive strike upon the American Pacific

---

4   The FBI picked up Yoshikawa on the day of the attack, but any incriminating evidence of his espionage had been destroyed. He eventually returned to Japan in August 1942 in a diplomatic prisoner exchange. Yoshikawa went into hiding after the war fearful of revenge by the American occupying force and Japanese citizens who partially blamed him for the war. Years later the Japanese government refused his pension request on the grounds that it never spied on anyone. Yoshikawa died jobless and penniless in a nursing home.

5   Yamamoto had been Japanese naval attaché in Washington DC and spoke fluent English. He was a graduate of Harvard University and had even visited the US Naval War College.

Fleet stationed in Hawaii circulated within Japanese Navy strategic thinkers.

The Japanese surmised that a surprise attack upon the US Pacific Fleet would so weaken American military strength in the Pacific and so demoralize both military and civilians that a decisive Japanese victory would be the only possible result.

During spring 1941, Commander Minoru Genda, a brilliant aviation staff officer, developed the Pearl Harbor attack details while other plans included simultaneous attacks on Malaya, the Philippines, Guam and Wake Islands, Hong Kong and the South Sea Islands.

The Japanese Striking Force was commanded by Vice Admiral Chuichi Nagumo[6] and included six aircraft carriers (*Akagi, Kaga, Soryu, Hiryu, Shokaku,* and *Zuikaku*) supported by two battleships, two heavy cruisers, nine destroyers, and refueling vessels. The 22-ship force assembled in Hitokappu Bay off the nearly uninhabited Eterofu Island, one of the Kurile Islands that ran north from Hokkaido toward the Soviet Kamchatka Peninsula. The fleet left the protected harbor on November 26. Their easterly course avoided the main shipping lanes and they maintained strict radio silence. The fleet encountered and sunk a Soviet fishing trawler to assure that no radio message of its presence was transmitted.

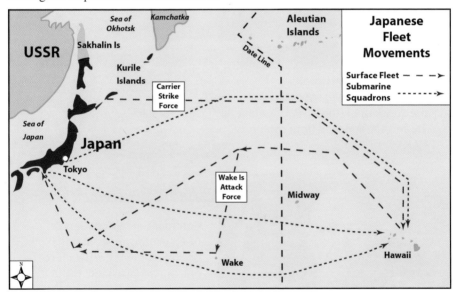

The early elimination of American fighter capability was crucial to Genda's plan because the Japanese could not risk engaging American aircraft in dog fights above the island or searching for the Japanese fleet. Thus the first bombs targeted the Army's Wheeler and Hickam Fields and the Navy reconnaissance aircraft on Ford Island. Kaneohe Naval Air Station, Bellows Field, and Ewa Marine Corps Station were secondary targets.

Genda selected the battleships and aircraft carriers east and west of Ford

---

6   The physically short, slight Nagumo was a peculiar choice to lead the mission. He was a naval torpedo expert and unfamiliar with aviation strategy and tactics.

Japanese commanders of the attack upon Pearl Harbor

Commander Mitsuo Fuchida (below, right) led the First Wave and remained throughout the attack to assess its success. NARA

Japanese Admiral Isoroku Yamamoto (above) conceptualized the attack upon the US Pacific Fleet by aircraft launched from carriers. NARA

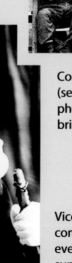

Commander Minoru Genda (seen center, above in this 1940 photo) planned the details of the brilliant aerial assault. NARA

Vice Admiral Chuichi Nagumo commanded the Strike Force even though he was not a supporter of the surprise attack plan, (left). NARA

Japanese pilots prepare to take off for the attack upon Pearl Harbor

Mitsubishi A6M (Zero) and Aichi D3A (Val) aircraft prepare to launch from the deck of the carrier *Shokaku* to attack Pearl Harbor. NARA

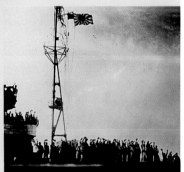

Nakajima B5N (Kate) torpedo bomber taking off from *Shokaku* to attack Pearl Harbor. Note the strong wing blowing the flags (above, left). The carrier's crew cheers their launch (above, right). NARA

Aichi D3A (Val) dive bombers prepare to take off from carrier *Akagi*; carrier *Soryu* in background. NARA

Island in the middle of Pearl Harbor as the naval primary targets. Torpedo planes would lead the attack against the outside row of ships followed by high-altitude and dive bombers against the inside row. The shallow waters of the harbor did not permit use of conventional torpedoes as they fell well below the surface before rising up and continuing on their course. Japanese engineers constructed and successfully tested wooden tail fins that attached to the torpedoes and held them to shallower depths. In order to pierce a battleship's thick armor, engineers reconstructed naval shells into bombs with reinforced surfaces such that they would not explode on impact but instead penetrate decks and detonate within the ships.

Washington DC

While the Japanese fleet steamed toward Hawaii, events in Washington were approaching their own conclusion. American and Japanese negotiators had been struggling to reach some accord over the disputes in Asia. Japan's designs upon Southeast Asia were well known; but PURPLE revealed nothing specific about Pearl Harbor. In a highly unusual action, Roosevelt transmitted a personal message directly to the Emperor requesting a peaceful resolution of differences. Tojo responded with a polite refusal.

On the morning of December 6, the Japanese Foreign Ministry sent a message to Japanese Ambassador Nomura to expect Dispatch #907, a 14-part reply to earlier American peace proposals. The 14th part arrived early the next morning along with curious instructions not to deliver the message until 13:00 (1:00 pm) December 7th Washington time, or 07:30 Hawaiian time. Its language implied war.

However, by 11:25 on 7 December Washington time, American cryptanalysts had already intercepted and decoded the message and had delivered MAGIC to General George Marshall, Army Chief of Staff. Thirty-three minutes later, Marshall directed a warning message to US commanders in Panama, Manila, San Francisco, and Hawaii regarding the Japanese ultimatum; unfortunately atmospheric disturbances prohibited the radio warning to Hawaii, so it was forwarded via commercial undersea cable.

The 13:00 delivery time of the 14-part message came and went, while Japanese embassy personnel continued to prepare the document.

US Forces on Oahu

American military leadership in Hawaii was divided between Pacific Fleet Admiral Husband Kimmel,[7] who held responsibility for the naval vessels, and Lieutenant General Walter Short,[8] commander of the Hawaiian Department which included the Army troops and Army Air Corps planes. Kimmel was focused upon possible submarine attacks; Short prepared for saboteurs – neither were concerned about air attacks.

---

7   Admiral Kimmel, from Henderson, Kentucky, was the son of a Civil War Confederate soldier. He graduated from the Naval Academy in 1904 to serve on several capital ships and in the War Department before taking up his post in Hawaii.

8   General Short, from the small town of Fillmore, Illinois, had attended the University of Illinois. As a junior officer he participated in the Mexican Expedition against Poncho Villa in 1916 and held staff positions during the First World War.

Hawaii, or more specifically the island of Oahu, was not without defenses. Coastal batteries guarded the shore line around the island as protection from a sea-borne invasion. The Army Air Corps provided bombardment and pursuit aircraft at Hickam and Wheeler Air Fields. Six other airstrips also held fighter planes, although many of the aircraft were inoperative due to shortages of replacement parts. Naval PBY flying boats patrolled surrounding waters from Ford Island. Five radar stations scanned the skies for incoming aircraft, although the technology was rather primitive at that time.

Pearl Harbor was home to eight Pacific Fleet battleships, three Pacific aircraft carriers, eight cruisers, fifty-six destroyers, thirty submarines, and other ships totaling 186 vessels in all. The battleships were moored in a double row east of Ford Island in what was known as Battleship Row. (See map on back cover.)

Admiral Husband Kimmel NHHC

The Battle of Taranto on the night of 11/12 November 1940 during which British carrier-based aircraft severely damaged the Italian fleet in that harbor demonstrated that surface ships were vulnerable to air bombardment. The US Navy felt it unsafe for battleships to leave the harbor without aircraft cover. However, the aircraft carrier USS *Lexington* was away carrying planes to Midway Island. Likewise, the USS *Enterprise* was returning after delivering fighter planes to Wake Island. The USS *Saratoga* was in a West Coast shipyard undergoing modifications. Thus, the fleet at sea would have no air cover. Pearl Harbor, on the other hand, was considered safe because it had extensive antiaircraft capability and fighter plane protection.

General Short had received the war warning of 27 November but inferred from its wording that the warning was primarily aimed at General Douglas McArthur, commander in the Philippines. His concern was the 130,000 Japanese descendants on the island and their potential for committing sabotage. Thus, his planes were not dispersed to protect against aerial bombardment as was the usual practice, but instead parked wingtip to wingtip along the runway aprons to be easily guarded against sabotage.

Pearl Harbor
7 December 1941

Midget Submarines (Part 1)

Twenty-five Japanese submarines approached Oahu including a Special Attack Unit of five submarines each transporting one 78-foot-long, two-man midget submarine. Their mission was to enter the harbor and destroy any American ship that survived the air attack. They were to then circle Ford Island counterclockwise, exit the harbor, and rendezvous with the mother submarines.

01:16 to 03:33: The five midget subs detached from their mother ships between 7 and 12 miles from the mouth of Pearl Harbor and set course for the naval base. Each carried two 1000 pound torpedoes. With only a few hours of power available from the midgets' batteries, the ten crewmen understood their probable fate.

03:42: The minesweeper USS *Condor* patrolled the waters 1 ¾ miles south of Pearl Harbor's entrance. Something in the darkness about fifty yards ahead off the port bow attracted the attention of Ensign Russell G McCloy, Officer of the Deck. He called to Quartermaster Second Class RC Uttrick and asked him what he thought. Uttrick peered through binoculars and said, 'That's a periscope, sir, and there aren't supposed to be any subs in this area.'[9]

03:57: The *Condor* reported the periscope sighting by blinker light to the destroyer USS *Ward*, which steamed to the area to investigate. Sonar sweeps found nothing. The *Ward* returned to its patrol.

06:30: An anti-torpedo curtain that spanned the entrance to Pearl Harbor began to separate to allow entry to the American supply ship USS *Antares* when its captain spotted a strange underwater craft having difficulty controlling its depth.

06:37: Lieutenant William Outerbridge, on his first day as commander of the destroyer USS *Ward*, spotted what looked like a submarine conning tower following the *Antares* 1,500 yards off the starboard quarter. Outerbridge had no doubt that the mysterious vessel was unfriendly.

06:45: The *Ward* closed to 100 yards and fired. The second shell hit at the junction of the hull and conning tower and the midget submarine sank leaving only a large oil slick on the surface. Depth charges followed.[10] The first American shots of the Second World War had been fired.

06:51: Outerbridge radioed the Naval District of the attack upon a submarine operating in the Oahu defensive area. [11]

07:10: Kimmel's staff, accustomed to numerous false alarms, asked for verification.

---

9   Lieutenant Russell Gifford McCloy of Seattle, Washington died on 9 August 1942 during the Battle of Savor Island and was buried at sea. He is commemorated on the Wall of the Missing in the Manila American Cemetery, Taguig City, Philippines.

10   In August 2002, a team from the University of Hawaii located the sub in 1,200 feet of water approximately 3 miles from the harbor entrance – almost exactly where the *Ward* recorded its attack.

11   Lieutenant William Outerbridge later commanded the destroyer *O'Brien*, which bombarded German defenses in Normandy on 6 June 1944. Reassigned to the Pacific, the *O'Brien* purposely fired upon and sank the USS *Ward*, Outerbridge's first command, after it had been severely damaged in a kamikaze attack in the Leyte Gulf. Outerbridge served in numerous naval capacities and ship commands before retiring in 1957 as a rear admiral. He died in 1986 at age 80.

First Wave

06:10: As the first light of dawn appeared, Japanese planes started to take off from the pitching, rolling deck of the aircraft carrier *Akagi*, flagship of the Japanese Fleet, led by Commander Mitsuo Fuchida. The First Wave held 183 attack aircraft each with a carefully assigned and practiced target. It included:

- 40 Nakajima B5N 'Kate' torpedo bombers carrying one 1760 pound torpedo targeted the outboard ships at Battleship Row;
- 51 Aichi D3A 'Val' dive bombers carried 500 pound bombs against American aircraft at Ford Island and Hickam Field to be followed by strafing runs with their three 7.7-mm machine guns;
- 49 Nakajima high altitude bombers carrying one 1700 pound, armor-piercing bomb or two 550 pound bombs targeted inboard ships at Battleship Row;
- 43 Mitsubishi A6M (Zero) fighters, already legendary for their quickness and nimble handling, flew against American planes using their two 20-mm wing-mounted cannon and two cowling-mounted 7.7-mm machine guns to maintain air supremacy over the battlefield.

The entire launch took only 15 minutes, then the aircraft headed south.

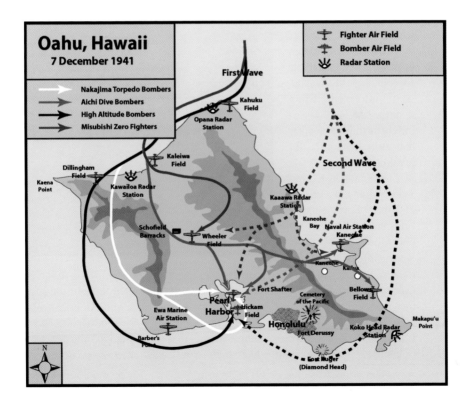

Opana Point

04:15: Opana Radar Station near the northern tip of Oahu, the only radar station operational that morning, turned on manned by two privates. In command was 19-year-old Joseph Lockard, of Williamsport, Pennsylvania. Lockard had been on a ship heading to Manila when it docked temporarily at Oahu three weeks earlier. He was reassigned to the rapidly expanding Aircraft Warning Signal Company. The second soldier was a trainee, Private George Elliot of Chicago who had two weeks experience as a plotter but was unfamiliar with radar operation.

07:00: The Opana Point station was scheduled to shut down, but trainee Elliot suggested they remain for more practice.

07:02: The station recorded large and unusual radar returns 132 miles north of Oahu. Lockard's first impression was that the equipment was faulty. A quick check proved otherwise. Elliot suggested that the pair inform the Information Center at headquarters in Fort Shafter. Lockard hesitated, but Elliot insisted and finally Lockard agreed.

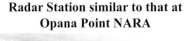

Radar Station similar to that at Opana Point NARA

07:10: Elliot tried the tactical line, but no one answered. He then used the administrative phone which was answered by the switchboard operator, Private Joseph McDonald, who informed Elliot that the six plotters at the Information Center had already left for breakfast.

07:15: Lieutenant Kermit Tyler was in charge of the Fort Shafter Information Center for only the second time. When informed of the radar returns, Tyler assumed they were an expected flight of B-17s flying from California on their way to Manila. It was well known throughout the islands that when radio station KGMB broadcast music all night, American planes were using the signal to home in on the islands. Tyler called Opana and told Lockard 'Well, don't worry about it' words that would haunt Tyler for the rest of his life.[12] The radar returns were then 88 miles distant.

12   A Navy Court of Inquiry in August 1942 determined that Tyler had been assigned to the Information Center with little or no training, no supervision, and no staff with which to work. Tyler was subsequently cleared of any wrong doing by the board and no disciplinary actions were taken against him. Lt Kermit Tyler went on to command fighter units in the Pacific. He retired at the rank of lieutenant colonel and died at his home in San Diego at age 96.

To their surprise that morning, Japanese pilots also heard the music. They recognized the distinctive Hawaiian beat and knew that American defenses had not been alerted. They also used the radio signal to home in on Oahu.

07:30: The very time that the Japanese ultimatum was scheduled to be delivered to the US State Department, the radar returns showed the Japanese attack force to be 45 miles from Oahu.

07:33: General Marshall's warning reached RCA offices in Honolulu, but because it was not labeled priority, it was not expedited to American headquarters. The Japanese First Wave was 35 miles away.

07:39: The Opana radar returns were at 20 miles, but then they were lost among radar reflections from nearby mountains; Lockard and Elliot shut Opana down.[13]

07:48: The Mitsubishi Zeros approached the northern tip of Oahu at Kahuku Point and flew down the north-south valley in the center of the island to come in north and west of Wheeler Field. Eleven Zeros from *Shokaku* and *Zuikaku* flew east to attack the naval air station at Kaneohe Bay, while Zeros from *Akagi* and *Kaga* continued toward Ewa Marime Air Station. Dive bombers from *Soryu* and *Hiryu* followed turning to approach Wheeler Field from the south.

07:50: Lt Tyler stepped outside the Information Center and saw planes approaching Pearl Harbor. He believed they were a Navy drill until Wheeler Field telephoned that the base was under attack. Tyler ordered McDonald to call back the Information Center staff.

07:51: Lieutenant Commander Shigeharu Murata's [14] torpedo planes divided into four attack groups. Two groups of eight planes each dove against Pearl Harbor from the west while two groups of twelve planes each arced over Hickam Field to attack Ford Island from the east.

07:53: Commander Fuchida ordered transmission of the signal 'Tora! Tora! Tora!' which literally means 'Tiger' but is also a contraction for the Japanese phrase 'We Attack.' The message informed his fleet that complete surprise had been achieved. Yamamoto was aboard his flagship battleship *Nagato* off the Japanese coast when his radio room intercepted the message. He sat motionless and expressionless.

08:04: KGMB interrupted the music to recall all Army, Navy, and Marine Corps personnel to duty. The call was repeated several times that morning before the station shut down.

Naval Air Station Kaneohe Bay

The earlier Kuwaaohe Army Military Reservation was reactivated in 1939 and was subjected to many name changes to include Camp Ulupau, and eventually named Fort Hase. That same year, the Navy established a base on the Mokapu

---

13   After the battle, Lockard was promoted, sent to Officers Candidate School, and given a Distinguished Service Medal. He spent the war at a radar station in the Aleutian Islands. Lockard died in 2012 at age 90.
George Elliot felt he never got credit for observing and insisting upon reporting the incoming Japanese planes. Elliot died in 2003 at age 85.

14   Shigeharu Murata later died in the Battle of Midway, 4 to 7 June 1942.

peninsula for long-range reconnaissance flights by PBY Catalina patrol seaplanes.

07:48: The base came under attack and, nearly defenseless without antiaircraft guns, all but three of the thirty-six Catalina seaplanes were damaged or destroyed. Aviation Ordnanceman Chief Petty Officer John Finn, a 15-year veteran in charge of base munitions, manned a .50-caliber machine gun taken from a burning plane and targeted an enemy plane as it emerged from billowing smoke. Eight rounds fired and the plane crashed into a hillside. The second wave caught Finn in a completely exposed

John Finn

section of the aircraft parking ramp. Although painfully wounded in the left arm and left foot, with shrapnel in his chest, abdomen, right elbow and thumb and cuts to his head, he continued to man his gun and vigorously returned the enemy's fire throughout the strafing and bombing attacks.[15]

Eighteen sailors and two civilians perished in the attack.

Ford Island

07:55: At Ford Island, nine dive bombers under Lieutenant Commander Kakuichi Takahashi[16] started their dives from 13,000 feet. Lieutenant Commander Logan Ramsey Sr, commander of the Navy's PBY amphibious Patrol Wing Two, had rushed from his home on Ford Island after being informed of a possible submarine sighting. Ramsey was working on a search plan when he looked out a window to see the first

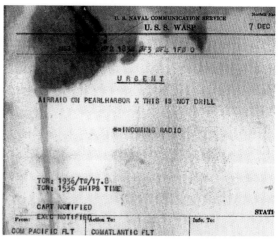

---

15   Chief Petty Officer John William Finn, son of a California plumber who dropped out of school after the seventh grade and enlisted in the Navy shortly before his seventeenth birthday, became the first Medal of Honor recipient in WW II for valor in his defense of the base. Finn was promoted to ensign in 1942 eventually retiring as a lieutenant. He died in 2010 at age 100 and is buried in Saint Carmel Cemetery, Campo Indian Reservation. He was the last surviving Medal of Honor recipient from the attack on Pearl Harbor, the oldest living recipient, and the only aviation ordnanceman to have ever received the award.

16   Kakuichi Takahashi died during the Battle of the Coral Sea, 4 to 8 May 1942.

dive bomber scream down on the sea plane ramp on the southern tip of Ford Island. A reckless U.S. pilot, he thought. Then he saw 'something black fall out of the plane' and realized it was a bomb. Ramsey ran to the radio room across the hall and ordered the transmission of an unencoded message to every ship and base.

07:58: Ford Island radio room sent that startling message 'AIR RAID ON PEARL HARBOR. STOP. THIS IS NOT DRILL.' The next two dive bombers blew Ramsey's PBY hanger and all the planes in it to pieces.[17]

Ewa Marine Corps Air Station

Ewa MCAS, originally designated Mooring Mast Field, was an early 1930s dirigible mooring station and emergency landing field. In 1940, the Navy began construction of Ewa Marine Corps Air Station and completed it the following year.

07:53: Nine Zeros led by Lieutenant Kiyokuma Okajima from *Hiryu* struck Ewa approaching from the northwest at altitudes as low as 20 feet. The planes began a devastating strafing of the parked Marine aircraft, buildings, and the original 100-foot dirigible mast topped by a flight control tower. Private William Turner and Technical Sergeant Emil Peters climbed into the rear cockpit of an SBD 'Dauntless' dive bomber and returned fire. Although both men were wounded, they are credited with shooting down one aircraft. Turner later died of his wounds.

The Zeros were joined later by dive bombers which had left Wheeler Field. After eight strafing runs, nine of eleven F4F fighters and eighteen of thirty-two SDB aircraft were destroyed. Casualties were four dead and thirteen wounded.

Hickam Field

Hickam Field was home to the 18th Bombardment Wing, which presented a potential threat to the Japanese Fleet. Fifty-nine bombers were stationed at the field, but only twenty were modern B-17s and only six of those were operational. Because of its high water table near the harbor, Hickam Field had no trenches, no air raid shelters, and no antiaircraft guns.

08:00: Seventeen dive bombers from the carrier *Shokaku* hit buildings and strafed people and planes at Hickam Field. Of the twenty-four men preparing obsolete B-18s for a scheduled training flight, twenty-two were killed and the other two men had their legs cut off from bullets or shrapnel.

Private First Class Frank Rom yelled a frantic warning to those enjoying Sunday breakfast in the new consolidated mess hall. Too late – a bomb crashed through the roof and 35 men died instantly. Dazed survivors gathered outside only to be hit by a fragmentation bomb leaving a pile of mangled bodies. Hale Makai Barracks was repeatedly strafed. Hangers 13 and 15 were destroyed by 500 pound bombs. Other bombs struck the chapel, guardhouse, fire station, and beer hall.

Hickam Field suffered 121 killed, 274 wounded, and 37 missing. Eighteen

---

17   Lieutenant Commander Logan Carlisle Ramsey Sr graduated from the Naval Academy in 1918. He retired in 1949 as a rear admiral. Ramsey died in 1972 and is buried in Arlington National Cemetery.

American air installations were among the first targets of the attack. Destroyed planes and hangers limited American ability to respond.

Naval aircraft on Ford land are destroyed while the USS Shaw explodes across the harbor. The sailor standing in the foreground has recently been identified as Adolph Kuhn. NARA

PBY patrol bomber burns outside a hanger at Naval Air Station Kaneohe while sailors attempt to extinguish the flames. NARA

Ford Island hanger burns from the aerial assault of dive bombers and fighter aircraft. NARA

Hickam Field was an early target of Japanese dive bombers

Aerial photograph of Hickam Field taken in September 1941 from 22,000 feet shows the runways, oil storage tanks (upper center) and Pearl Harbor's narrow exit channel, (left). NARA

A B-17 stands at Hickam Field while hangers burn in the distance, (inset, below). NARA

The burnt-out shell of Hickam Field's hanger #11 displays the devastation of the attack, (below). NARA

of the planes were totally destroyed, twenty-two damaged. Only nineteen aircraft survived the attack.

Wheeler Field / Schofield Barracks

The Army's fighter base at Wheeler Field held fifty-two operational, modern P-40s and thirty operational, but obsolete, P-36 and P-26 fighter aircraft of the 14th Pursuit Wing. The base had been on an alert status all week long until Saturday morning. The alert was called off after morning inspection and all personnel not on week end duty received a pass. Planes were left lined up, as ordered, wing tip to wing tip on the ramp in front of the four large plane hangars. One million rounds of machine-gun ammunition was locked in the ordnance building as another anti-sabotage measure. Wheeler also had no trenches, no air raid shelters, and no antiaircraft guns.

08:02: The first Japanese dive bombers from the *Zuikaku*'s 16th Attack Unit peeled off to strafe the barracks and airplanes parked along the runway apron. The hanger was soon ablaze with ammunition exploding like firecrackers as twenty-five dive-bombers dropped approximately thirty-five bombs.

Second Lieutenant Francis Gabreski woke up in Schofield Barracks around 08:00 when he heard a screaming whine, explosions, and machine gun fire. After waking other pilots, the partially dressed group ran toward the Wheeler Field flight line to manually push planes away from burning buildings and flaming aircraft. Twelve pilots got airborne and headed for Pearl Harbor where they underwent friendly antiaircraft fire. [18]

08:10: The Japanese 3rd and 4th Fighter Units again strafed the parked aircraft, barracks, Post Exchange (PX), admin building, and the golf course while ruptured gasoline tanks spewed aviation fuel towards undamaged aircraft.

08:14: Machine guns on the field's tennis courts commenced firing at the attacking aircraft and one Mitsubishi Zero faltered before crashing.

08:25: At the adjacent Schofield Barracks, Lieutenant Stephen Saltzman, communications officer of the 98th Coast Artillery Regiment, and Sergeant Lowell V Klatt heard the scream of aircraft pulling out of dives. Both men grabbed BARs and two magazines, ran outside, and fired while the enemy fired back. Finally, two planes rose, one to the left and one to the right, to clear nearby high tension wires. The left plane, struck by Klatt's machine gun fire, lost altitude and crashed. [19]

---

18   Second Lieutenant Francis Gabreski, son of Polish immigrants from Oil City Pennsylvania, graduated from Notre Dame University where he developed an interest in flying. Gabreski became the top American fighter ace in Europe with 34 ½ victories. He crashed his plane during a strafing run over a German airfield on his last mission before a scheduled return to the states. He spent the remainder of the war as a POW in Stalag I. Gabreski also became a jet fighter ace in Korea becoming one of only seven pilots to ace in two wars. After a stellar command career, he retired in 1967. He died in 2002 at age 83 and is buried in Calverton National Cemetery in eastern Long Island, New York. He and his wife were married for 48 years and raised nine children. Two of his three sons became career Air Force pilots.

19   Sergeant Lowell Vincent Klatt was awarded a Silver Star for fearlessly facing and shooting down an attacking aircraft. Klatt died in 2007 at age 94.
Lieutenant Stephen Ginns Saltzman also received a Silver Star. Saltzman transferred to the US Army Air Corps. While flying a P-38 Lightning over Europe, he suffered injuries when enemy antiaircraft

After their bombing run, the dive bombers returned four or five times to strafe the field sending machine gun bullets through the barracks and killing approximately 200 soldiers.

08:45: First Lieutenant Lew Sanders, commanding officer of the 46th Pursuit Squadron, led four P-36s into the air. The Information Center, now staffed and operational, reported numerous enemy planes (Second Wave) over Kaneohe Bay and Bellows Field. Sanders and Second Lieutenant Gordon Sterling engaged two Zeros in a four plane dive – Zero, Sterling's plane, Zero, and Sanders' plane. It was commonly believed that all three bullet-hole-riddled planes crashed and only Sanders was able to pull out of the dive; however, the aircraft entered a cloud bank and post-war Japanese records show that the two Japanese pilots were able to make their escape. Only Sterling died. [20]

Casualties at Wheeler totaled thirty-three killed and seventy-five wounded. Of the 233 aircraft assigned to the Hawaiian Department Air Force, eighty-three were totally destroyed.

USS *Utah,* USS *Raleigh* and USS *Detroit*

At the same time that the dive bombers struck the two airfields, sixteen of Murata's Nakajima torpedo bombers of the 3rd and 4th Torpedo Attack Units spearheaded the attack upon ships moored on the northeast side of Ford Island. Their intended targets were the aircraft carriers normally berthed on this side of the island. They found only the decommissioned *Utah* and two light cruisers.

The USS *Utah*, a member of the *Florida* class of dreadnought[21] battleships launched in December 1909 and completed in August 1911, held a main battery of ten 12-inch guns in five twin gun turrets. During the First World War, the *Utah* protected North Atlantic convoys from German surface ships. In 1931 the ship was decommissioned and used for a decade as a gunnery practice target. Heavy wood beams erected to protect the crew may have given the vessel the appearance of an early aircraft carrier and thus fooled Japanese pilots into thinking it was an American carrier.

The aging light cruisers *Raleigh* and *Detroit* were sister ships that had been in service since the early 1920s. They stood in stark contrast to the more modern designs of the newer cruisers in Pearl Harbor at the time. Their four smokestacks and tall forward tripod mast made them look more like a large World War I-era destroyer

---

fire struck his cockpit. The force of the explosion shattered the top of the aircraft's control column and broke both his right wrist and one of the fingers of his right hand as well as wounding him in the left arm and thigh. He managed to get back to England, but immediately lost consciousness upon landing from loss of blood. He was awarded the Distinguished Flying Cross for his daring. Saltzman flew in Korea and Vietnam before retiring with the rank of colonel. He died in 2000 at age 81 and is buried in Arlington National Cemetery.

20   Lieutenant Gordon H Sterling from Connecticut is listed as Missing in Action in the Court of the Missing in the National Cemetery of the Pacific and on a memorial stone at Arlington National Cemetery.
Lieutenant Lewis M Sanders, a barnstorming pilot before joining the Air Corps, is thought to be the first pilot to shoot down an enemy plane on 7 December. He remained in the Air Force and retired as a colonel. He died in 1984 at age 77.

21   A dreadnought is defined as having more heavy-caliber guns than previous ships and steam turbine propulsion.

than a light cruiser.

07:56: Ensign Donald Korn, a graduate of Indiana University Law School and a Navy pilot aboard cruiser USS *Raleigh*, was turning over the deck to his replacement when he noticed planes flying down the valley along the center of Oahu. After passing over Pearl City, he watched one group headed for ships anchored west of Ford Island at an altitude of only 50 feet. Two planes headed for the USS *Utah*, one plane each headed for USS *Detroit* and USS *Raleigh*.

08:01: Aboard the *Utah*, the first torpedo hit the ship on the port side. It was about 5 or 8 minutes before someone hollered that the Japanese were attacking. The ship suffered two more torpedo hits and started to list. While his shipmates evacuated, Chief Watertender Peter Tomich remained below securing the boilers and assuring that all the men had gotten out of the engineering spaces.[22]

Lieutenant Commander Solomon Isquith, engineering officer, made an inspection to make sure men were out and nearly became trapped himself. As the ship began to turn over, he found an escape hatch blocked. While he was attempting to escape through a porthole during the ever-increasing list of the ship, the bed upon which he was standing slipped out from beneath him. Fortunately, Lieutenant Commander Lindley Winser, the ship's communications officer, outside grabbed Isquith's arm and pulled him through at the last instant.[23]

08:05: A torpedo hit the light cruiser USS *Raleigh* opposite its second funnel. With a shattering roar, the entire ship lurched and the forward engine room flooded. A launch preparing to take men to Sunday services splintered and disintegrated throwing its passengers into the water. Despite the damage, the *Raleigh's* crew was able to keep the ship upright by counter flooding while its gunners maintained antiaircraft fire at the attacking planes shooting down five enemy aircraft.

08:12: Tug boats attached lines and attempted to right the *Utah* but water filled the below sea level compartments too quickly and the vessel capsized.

Fireman John Vaessen, remained at his post in the dynamo room assuring the ship had enough power to keep her lights going as long as possible. He recalls the day:

> I crawl down in there. So I take the wrench and I rap on the bottom. I said, 'Gee, it sounds like it's out of [the] water. This is a pretty good sign.' So I hit it some more. I didn't know we were at war. I mean, this was unbeknownst to me. So, anyway, I rapped on the bottom, rapped and rapped. You know, your hopes are always up, so I rapped and rapped. Gee, I got the damnedest blister on my hand, but I kept rapping anyway.

Hearing knocking from the ship's hull, machinists grabbed welding torches

---

22   Originally Petar Herceg Tonić from Herzegovina, Chief Watertender Peter Tomich joined the US Army in 1917, later transferring to the US Navy. Tomich, 48 years old, was posthumously awarded a Medal of Honor for his sacrifice. He is commemorated on the Courts of the Missing in the National Cemetery of the Pacific.

23   Lieutenant Commander Solomon Silas Isquith, the second of nine children from Brooklyn, New York and a Naval Academy graduate, served in both world wars before retiring in 1950 at two-star rank. Isquith was awarded a Navy Cross for his daring and leadership in leading rescue efforts on other ships in the harbor. He later commanded salvage operation in the stricken harbor. He died in 1969 at age 73 and is buried in Arlington National Cemetery.

and cut escape holes. Ten men clambered from the would-be tomb. The last man out was Fireman Vaessen carrying a flashlight and his wrench. [24]

USS *Utah* remains at Ford Island to this day – still capsized. Sixty-four of *Utah*'s crew died.

The torpedo aimed at the USS *Detroit* missed.

USS *Ogala* and USS *Helena*

The USS *Ogala* was originally built for overnight coastal passenger service between Boston and New York City. In November 1917, the ship was purchased by the US Navy and converted to a minelayer for use against German submarines in the North Sea. After the war, she served as a seaplane tender and minelayer. The USS *Helena* was a light cruiser completed shortly before the attack.

07:57: Most of the torpedo bombers ignored the lesser ships west of Ford Island and continued east. Admiral William R Furlong strolled along the deck of the antique minelayer *Ogala* waiting for his breakfast to be prepared. Third Torpedo Attack Unit's commander, Lieutenant Takashi Nagai released his torpedo. A sailor pointed Furlong's attention toward the torpedo's wake, but the admiral could only watch helplessly as it went under the shallow-draft *Ogala* and struck the *Helena* which was moored inboard at Ten Ten Pier, where the USS *Pennsylvania* was normally berthed. The torpedo hit the *Helena* amidship near the engine room. The force of the explosion burst the *Ogala*'s hull.

08:01: The *Helena* began to flood but the slight list was contained by counter-flooding. Wiring to the main and secondary gun batteries was severed, but prompt action by damage control brought the forward diesel generator up within minutes, making power available to all gun mounts and for fire fighting. With attacking planes flying overhead, the crew broke out ammunition and sent up antiaircraft fire.

08:28: The *Ogala* was listing as its engine room flooded and water rapidly spread aft. Tugs towed the ship astern of the *Helena* to clear the range for the Helena's guns. Heavy antiaircraft fire from the *Helena* repelled further Japanese attackers and they veered away.

10:00: Admiral Furlong ordered the *Ogala* abandoned as the stricken ship rolled toward the dock. For the Japanese, it was a double victory.

The *Helena* attempted to get underway, but damage to the infrastructure was too severe and the attempt was abandoned. [25]

General Walter Short was having breakfast with his wife when the planes struck. Hearing the rolling explosions from torpedoes striking the *Utah* and *Helena*, Short walked to his back porch for a look. Seeing the rising columns of smoke, he ran to his office and, at 0810, ordered his command to change from anti-sabotage alert to

---

24   For his actions during the attack, Fireman John B Vaessen was awarded the Navy Cross. As of 2017, he still lives in California at age 101.

25   After repairs in California, the USS *Helena* rejoined the Pacific Fleet and participated in sea battles protecting the Guadalcanal amphibious landings in 1942. She was sunk by three surface-fired torpedoes at the Battle of Kula Gulf in 1943. The first torpedo blew off the bow and the ship sank in 22 minutes with the loss of 168 lives.

anti-invasion alert. He and his command staff evacuated to the underground command center in Aliamanu Crater. [26]

USS *Arizona*

The Pennsylvania-class USS *Arizona* was launched in June 1915, but was not completely operational until March 1917. It served in the Atlantic Fleet during the First World War. A modernization program was completed in 1931 when the *Arizona* was flagship for a battleship division in the Atlantic.

07:56: Seven sailors from the repair ship USS *Vestal* had taken a launch across the channel into the Southeast Loch where at they witnessed a single file of torpedo planes of the 1st and 2nd Torpedo Attack Units approaching Battleship Row from over Hickam Field so low that they clipped the tops of the palm trees. Once over the water, they dropped to 20 feet while the fighters circled overhead.

08:00: Planes dropped torpedoes aimed at the USS *Arizona* and peeled to the right over the USS *Nevada*'s fantail where the ship's band had just began playing the Star Spangled Banner. The plane's rear gunners sprayed the *Nevada* with bullets but missed the band and the Marine color guard. The band hurriedly completed the National Anthem and then scattered.

Two torpedoes aimed at the *Arizona* struck the service ship USS *Vestal*, which was anchored outboard of the battle wagon.[27] Then a high altitude bomb shattered the deck between No 4 and No 6 guns. The quarter deck was engulfed in flames; shipmates grabbed hoses to fight the fires – no water pressure; sailors shouted into phones for water – but there was no power. Internal explosions threw them to the deck.

08:10: For a few brief minutes, fires raged across the decks of the Arizona. Then, the ship died. An armor piercing bomb dropped by pilot Tadashi Kusumi from the *Hiryu* struck near the forward powder magazine igniting one million pounds of explosives. A loud 'whoom' sent huge tongues of flame in all directions. The concussion blew men off the *Arizona*, off the *Nevada*, and off other nearby ships. Flaming debris started fires on the nearby *Tennessee*. Even Commander Fuchida in his plane 10,000 feet above felt the turbulence.

The blast vaporized men and left parts of bodies hanging from the rigging. The forward part of the ship was blown away causing the foremast and forward superstructure to collapse into the emptiness. Turrets #1 and #2, now without support, dropped twenty feet. Lights went out and smoke swept through the corridors. Stunned sailors staggered across decks littered with burning bodies mixed with burning debris. Temporarily blinded men groped forward seeking help. A husky cook sat staring at the blood pumping from the stump of his severed leg.

---

26   A bunker complex beneath Aliamanu crater existed on 7 December as an invasion command post. The extensive tunnels and twenty rooms now lie sealed and store pesticide. Government housing is on the surface of what is now the Aliamanu Military Reservation.

27   Controversy continues about one of these torpedoes passing under the *Vestal* and striking the *Arizona*. At the time most observers claimed to witness a torpedo hit, but Navy divers inspecting the wreckage recently state that they found no evidence of an inward explosion on the vessel's hull as might be expected from a torpedo hit.

Japanese planes attack the US Pacific Fleet at Ford Island

Photo taken by a Japanese airman early in the attack upon Battleship Row shows a water plume from the explosion of a torpedo against the USS *Oklahoma*. A torpedo bomber is seen as it turns through the smoke. Another 'Kate' turns over the Navy Yard (top right). The USS *Utah* is already listing (far left of photo). The oil tank farm is visible on the upper right. NARA

USS *Arizona* is sunk and in flames. The USS *Tennessee* and USS *West Virginia* are side by side behind the smoldering wreck. NARA

Battleships burn from repeated hits by bombs and torpedos

USS *California* lists and starts to sink. Note the Ford Island water tower to the right, (right photo). NARA

A bow-on view of the comparatively lightly damaged battleship USS *Maryland* with the burning USS *West Virginia* behind and the capsized USS *Oklahoma* adjacent, (below). NARA

The USS *Nevada* lies beached after the attack. Its crew tackles the fires. NARA

Burning hulks are all that remain of the US Pacific Fleet

The USS *Utah* strains at its mooring ropes before capsizing. NARA

Burning oil coats the harbor water. NARA

View from Ten Ten Pier. Visible are battleships *Maryland*, the capsized *Oklahoma*, the *Tennesse,* and the *Arizona*'s masts. NARA

Captain Franklin Van Valkenburgh was on the navigation bridge directing the ship's defenses when the violent explosion threw the three occupants to the floor. Flames came through the bridge windows which had been previously broken by gunfire. Captain Van Valkenburgh was never seen again and his body was never recovered. Rear Admiral Isaac C Kidd was last seen on the signal bridge before the massive explosion. [28]

Six sailors were trapped on the portside antiaircraft director by the flames below. They were badly burned and fearful that they might not escape. Aboard the USS *Vestal* Petty Officer Joseph George spotted the waving victims and threw them a line. While Japanese pilots strafed survivors and with the oil-covered water below in flames, the six men went hand-over-hand to safety onto the *Vestal*. Two of the men died later that day in the hospital.

Marine Major Alan Shapley was blown out of the foremast and catapulted into the water. Regaining his senses, he was swimming toward Ford Island when he found Corporal Earl C Nightingale struggling to stay afloat. Shapley had the young corporal put his arms around his shoulders. Bombs sent shock waves through the water and, as both men slipped beneath the surface, Nightingale saluted his commanding officer. The water was only a few feet deep and Shapley pushed up pulling Nightingale with him to the pipeline connecting the ship to Ford Island. Both men made shore.

Major Shapley wandered around Ford Island wearing only a long red scarf given to him on shore by the embarrassed wife of a Navy acquaintance. The air was permeated with the smell of burning flesh. He headed toward the airfield in search of a machine gun. Eventually a chief petty officer escorted the still dazed Marine officer to a nearby building, gave him some clothes, and guided him to a dugout.[29]

08:20: Lieutenant Commander Samuel Fuqua, although knocked unconscious by a bomb blast, led firefighting efforts on the aft portion of the ship when the massive explosion sent a wall of flames 500 feet into the air. Realizing the source of such a violent explosion and because the ship's antiaircraft guns had fallen silent, Fuqua gave the order to abandon ship as burning oil quickly surrounded the ship vessel.[30]

The *Arizona* sank in 9 minutes. The Arizona carried a complement of 1,512 men; 1,177 were killed – almost one-half of the total fatalities that day. Nine hundred men were entombed in its flooded compartments – never to be rescued. Twenty-three

---

28   Captain Franklin Van Valkenburgh, whose ancestors fought in the Revolutionary and Civil Wars, received the Medal of Honor for his devotion to duty. His body was never recovered; only his ring was found among the wreckage on the flag bridge.
Rear Admiral Isaac C Kidd was the highest ranking casualty at Pearl Harbor and was the first Navy flag officer killed in the war. His body was never recovered. Kidd was awarded a Medal of Honor for courageously discharging his duties.

29   Major Alan Shapley, a Naval Academy graduate, was awarded a Silver Star for gallantry in Pearl Harbor and a Navy Cross for heroism during the Battle of Guam. Later in the war Shapley commanded the 2nd Marine Raider Regiment, an elite commando-type force. Shapley retired in 1962 as a lieutenant general.

30   Lieutenant Commander Samuel G Fuqua was awarded a Medal of Honor for his efforts in saving survivors of the *Arizona*. Fuqua commanded several ships during the war finally retiring in 1953 as a rear admiral. Fuqua died at age 87 and is buried in Arlington National Cemetery.

pairs of brothers died as did a father and his son.

USS *Vestal*

The Navy repair ship USS *Vestal* was moored outboard the *Arizona* performing routine maintenance. Officer of the Deck, Chief Warrant Officer Fred Hall ordered General Quarters the moment the first Japanese planes flew overhead.

08:05: The ship was struck by two bombs, one of which penetrated the superstructure, mess deck, and detonated in a steel storeroom. The second bomb penetrated through the entire ship and lodged unexploded in the harbor mud.

Samuel Fuqua NHHC

08:10: The *Arizona* explosion blew one hundred men off the *Vestal*. Tons of debris fell upon the ship; parts of the *Arizona* were mingled with parts of bodies of its crew. Ensign BC Hesser, still aboard the *Vestal*, saw men standing at the *Arizona*'s gun stations surrounded by smoke and fire. Suddenly they all fell – dead.

Commander Cassin Young rapidly organized offensive action when the enemy struck, personally taking charge of one of *Vestal*'s 3-inch antiaircraft guns. He was blown into the harbor water by the *Arizona*'s explosion, but swam through burning oil to reboard and get the vessel underway. [31]

08:45: The crew axed the mooring lines tying the *Vestal* to the burning *Arizona* and the *Vestal* proceeded through the harbor.

09:50: Bomb damage had destabilized the ship and Young ordered it grounded near Aiea landing.

USS *West Virginia*

08:08: The USS *West Virginia* sounded General Quarters as the first torpedo struck directly beneath a casemate. Seaman Robert Bonton, after being thrown to the deck, regained his feet and looked up to see bombs fall 'like snowflakes.' Two more torpedoes hit forward on the port side. A heavy explosion followed and the

---

31   Commander Cassin Young's heroism was recognized with the Medal of Honor. Young died in 1942 while commanding the heavy cruiser USS *San Francisco* during an engagement with a Japanese battleship near Guadalcanal. He was awarded the Navy Cross for this action. Young was buried at sea and is commemorated on the Wall of the Missing in Manila American Cemetery, Taguig City, Philippines.

ship started to list to port as compartments flooded. Everything loose began a slow slide to port – tables, chairs, plotting boards, and desks. Men trapped below deck drowned as the sealed compartments slowly flooded. Captain Mervyn Bennion doubled up hit by a bomb fragment and mortally wounded. Mess Attendant 2nd Class Doris Miller, a well-built man and the ship's heavyweight boxing champion, rushed to Bennion's aid. The captain's injuries, however, dictated that he not be moved. He continued to follow the battle until he died.[32]

Seaman Doris Miller USN

Two officers, Miller, and a seaman manned idle machine guns on the conning tower. Miller gleefully opened fire on the Japanese planes. Later, Miller carried men to the quarter deck saving their lives.[33]

Gunnery Officer Lieutenant Claude Ricketts, on his own authority, directed counter flooding and the *West Virginia*, hit by six torpedoes and two bombs, slowly swung back to starboard and settled down into the harbor mud.

Signalman Gene Merrill volunteered to go below as a member of a rescue team. He located body after body looking for signs of life. Rising salt water covered in oil forced him to evacuate. Topside he found the battle was over. Merrill was taken to a receiving station for treatment.[34]

Sixty sailors remained trapped below decks and perished; of those, three sailors sat hopelessly in the pump room crossing off sixteen days on a calendar before expiring. In all, 106 sailors aboard the *West Virginia* died.

USS *Tennessee*

USS *Tennessee*, a 32,300-ton battleship, was built at the New York Navy Yard and commissioned in June 1920. Moored inboard of the USS *West Virginia*, the USS *Tennessee* was shielded from the torpedo attacks that so devastated the outboard

---

32   Captain Mervyn Bennion was awarded a Medal of Honor posthumously for conspicuous dedication to duty. Bennion is buried near his home in Salt Lake City.

33   In May 1942, Doris Miller, son of a sharecropper from Waco, Texas who had enlisted in 1939 at age 19, was awarded the Navy Cross, the first black man to be so honored in the Pacific in the Second World War. Nearly two years after Pearl Harbor on 24 November, the escort carrier USS *Liscome Bay* was sunk by a Japanese submarine in the Gilbert Islands. Miller was among the 626 men to die in the action. Miller is buried in Doris Miller Memorial Park on the banks of the Brazos River in Waco. A nine-foot bronze statue was unveiled 7 December 2017 at the memorial.

34   Signalman Benjamin E Merrill subsequently served on three destroyers which saw action in the Pacific. After serving twenty-four years in the Navy, Merrill retired to later graduate from law school.

vessels. The ship opened fire with .50-caliber machine guns about five minutes after the first attack. Debris from the *Arizona* explosion was thrown on the quarterdeck of the *Tennessee* and intense heat from the fires aboard the *Arizona* started fires in the stern and port quarter of the ship. The *Tennessee* was hit by two bombs, which damaged #2 and #3 gun turrets. Splinters flew in all directions, one being responsible for Captain Bennion's injuries on the *West Virginia*.

USS *Oklahoma*

07:56: A three-plane group led by *Akagi* squadron commander Lieutenant Jinichi Goto released their torpedoes toward the USS *Oklahoma* ripping a 140-foot-long hole in the port side. The second of those torpedoes put out the lights; the third hit the middle of the ship. Antiaircraft guns were silent because the ammunition boxes were locked.

08:06: The ship started to roll to port and 1,400-pound shells rolled across the handling rooms sweeping men and materiel before them. Ladders were stuffed with men going down to escape the topside explosions against men going up chased by the rising flood waters.

08:10: Five planes from the carrier *Soryu* unloaded their 1700-pound bombs upon the badly listing *Oklahoma*. One hit between two gun turrets and penetrated into an ammunition room. Flames shot out of holes in the ship.

Commander Jesse Kenworthy Jr, the executive officer, recalls attempting to reach the conning tower across a deck awash with water and oil when he felt another major explosion. The list was at 25 degrees when Kenworthy ordered the ship abandoned over the starboard side. He then stepped over the starboard rail and walked up the side onto the bottom of the ship.

Ensign Francis Flaherty, a 22-year-old from south central Michigan, had enlisted in the Naval Reserve after graduating from the University of Michigan and one year later found himself

Ensign Francis Flaherty and Seaman James Ward USN

aboard the *Oklahoma*. After the torpedoes struck the ship's electrical power was lost. Flaherty was in one of the gun turrets as the ship started to roll over. He remained in the turret providing battery powered light so the turret crew could escape. Similarly, 20–year-old Seaman 1st Class James Ward from Springfield, Ohio also held illumination in a turret so his shipmates could make their escape.[35]

---

35   Both men died at their posts and received Medals of Honor for their personal sacrifices. Fifteen Medals of Honor were awarded for actions at Pearl Harbor that day – ten of them posthumously. Less than two years later, two destroyer escort ships were commissioned and named in Flaherty's (DE-135) and Ward's honor (DE-243).

08:14: The Oklahoma was bottom up with her mast and superstructure jammed into the harbor's mud bottom. Men immersed in water and oil were trapped in the capsized hull. Some collapsed from breathing oil fumes while three brothers, Tom, Pat and Terry Armstrong, all made it off the ship and into the water.

Trapped men hollered for help as the compartments slowly flooded. Small group scrambled to reach ever higher (actually lower) areas of the ship chased by the increasing water level. Seaman Albert Ellis went up to the top of a ladder to find it barred by a locked door. He beat off the lock with a wrench to find a black, but dry room. The men plugged the air vents with clothes and waited.[36]

The ship's chaplain, Father Aloysius Schmitt, was too hefty to exit by the open fifteen-inch porthole; he helped shove sailor after sailor though the small opening. Seaman Adolph Kuhn made it out, but his unnamed friend was a bigger challenge. As Father Al and others shoved and pulled, the man's ribs were heard cracking. Despite his painful injuries, the sailor shouted for his friends to keeping pulling. He made it.[37]

Marine Private Ray Turpin was one of the helpers. His turn came and he slipped through the opening into harbor water covered in three inches of oil. Turpin tried to shimmy up the mooring line from the *Oklahoma* to the *Maryland*, but the *Oklahoma* was pulling the nearby ship away from the quay. As Turpin neared the ship, an officer gave the order to axe the line. The sailor hesitated because of the fifteen men doing as Turpin was, but upon a second command he whacked the line free. Turpin and the others fell fifteen feet into the harbor. Turpin untangled himself from the coil of mooring rope as exhaustion overcame him. A sailor threw him a line and dragged him to safety on the *Maryland*'s deck. There Turpin found his fellow marines firing a four-barrel, antiaircraft machine gun at the Japanese planes. He finally was able to join in the fight.[38]

For the next 36 hours, welders swarmed the upturned *Oklahoma*'s hull frantically trying to cut escape holes in the ship's steel plate. Thirty-two crew members were rescued from inside the hull, but others died from the smoke from welding torches. Despite their efforts, 429 men were entombed and remained so until 1943 when the ship was raised and their remains were buried in unmarked mass graves in the National Memorial Cemetery of the Pacific.[39]

USS *Maryland*

USS *Maryland*, a 32,600-ton Colorado class battleship, was built at Newport News, Virginia and commissioned in July 1921. The *Maryland*, moored inboard of the USS *Oklahoma*, became the target of the high-altitude bombers' second pass. All

---

36   Seaman Albert Ellis of Portland Oregon survived his ordeal.

37   Father Aloysius Schmitt could not escape and became the first chaplain to die in the Second World War. He was awarded the Navy and Marine Corps Medal posthumously.

38   Private Raymond John Turpin, from Waterloo, Alabama, was one of 10 children from a family so poor that it kept food cold by putting it in the creek behind their home. Turpin served as part of the occupation force in Japan and in Korea. He died in 2009 at age 88. He is survived by three children, eleven grandchildren, and eleven great-grandchildren.

39   Spurred by a researcher and Pearl Harbor survivors, in 2015 the Defense Department announced plans to exhume an estimated 388 of the Oklahoma's unknowns. Sixty-one rusty caskets were retrieved from 45 graves. The process of identification continues.

antiaircraft batteries were promptly manned early in the attack, possibly destroying the first two planes that approached the *Maryland* and the *Oklahoma*. They then focused upon the dive bombing and strafing attacks which followed the torpedo attack. Nonetheless, an armor piercing bomb crashed into the hull and a second bomb exploded on the deck. Shipfitter 1st Class Andrew Joseph Geiser, among the first to arrive at his battle station, flooded the aviation gasoline stowage thereby probably avoiding a devastating explosion from an enemy bomb that struck the forecastle directly above that very compartment.[40]

USS *California*

08:05: Admiral Kimmel arrived at Fleet HQ to witness two torpedoes hit the port side of the USS *California*. Kimmel continued to observe events motionless and glassy-eyed from the tower of the submarine base. While doing so, a spent .50-caliber bullet crashed through the glass and harmlessly struck Kimmel in the chest. Kimmel is said to have turned to his communications officer and said, 'It would have been merciful had it killed me.' He was removed from his command ten days later.

08:20 to 08:30: The *California* suffered four bomb hits with one bomb penetrating the main deck and exploding. The ship listed 8 degrees to port. In the flooded forward air compressor compartment Machinist's Mate 1st Class Robert Scott refused to leave his post. 'This is my station and I will stay and give them air as long as the guns are going.' He died doing his job.[41]

Helping to pass that ammunition was Chief Radioman Thomas Reeves, a career Navy man who originally enlisted during the First World War. Discharged in 1921, he re-enlisted months later and found himself on the USS *California* that morning. Reeves remained in a burning passageway to pass ammunition by hand until he fell unconscious and died. [42]

Ensign Edgar Fain directed counter flooding to prevent the ship from capsizing and it settled with only its superstructure above water. One hundred and five sailors were dead.

B-17 Flight

08:20: A squadron of fourteen B-17s, led by Major Truman Landon, a West Point graduate from Maryville, Missouri, arrived after a 14-hour flight from San Francisco. They were low on gas, their guns were packed in preservative cosmolene, and they had no ammunition or gunners. At first, Landon thought that the Japanese Zeros were an Army Air Corps welcoming committee. The squadron attempted landings at Hickam. As Landon banked for his approach, the Hickam Field Tower warned, 'You have three Japs on your tail.' Landon

---

40   The USS *Maryland* was fully repaired and operational only thirteen days later.

41   Twenty-six-year-old Robert R Scott was awarded a Medal of Honor for his conspicuous devotion to duty and extraordinary courage. He is buried in Arlington National Cemetery.

42   Forty-seven-year-old Thomas Reeves was also awarded a Medal of Honor for his sacrifice. He now lies in the National Memorial Cemetery of the Pacific.

landed despite numerous bullet hits to his plane.[43]

Burned-B-17C NARA

The second plane to land had magnesium flares on board which were hit by Japanese bullets. The flares burned off the rear half of the plane. It landed anyway, but Dr William Schick was killed by a bullet as he ran to safety becoming the only B-17 fatality. Japanese planes strafed the bombers on the ground three or four times, but the empty fuel tanks became a blessing as the sturdy craft absorbed the hits but did not explode.

Captain Richard Carmichael led a squadron of six more B-17s. Two utilized every foot of runway to land at the fighter strip at Haleiwa, three landed at Hickam, and 1st Lieutenant Frank Bostrom landed his B-17 on the Kahuku Golf Course.

Twenty B-17s were already at Hickam but only two got into the air to search for the Japanese carriers. They were sent south where they found the approaching Enterprise and almost bombed their own ship.

Second Wave

Twenty minutes after the first wave departed, the second wave of Japanese planes arrived. The torpedo bombers were dispensed with, Genda figuring that they were too slow and too exposed to survive a now aroused opponent. Led by Commander Shigekazu Shimazaki, the second force totaled 170 air craft: 80 dive bombers, 54 high altitude bombers, and 36 fighters. [44]

Bellows Field

The base was created in 1917 as the Waimanalo Military Reservation and renamed *Bellows Field* in 1933 after Lieutenant Franklin Barney Bellows, a First World War hero.[45]

08:30: A lone B-17, piloted by 1st Lieutenant Robert H Richards of the 38th Reconnaissance Squadron, approached the air strip. Richards could not make Hickam Field because Japanese Zeros had riddled his aircraft from nose to tail, shot away the ailerons, and severely wounded three crew members. He touched down halfway along the strip. Knowing he would not be able to stop, Richards retracted the wheels and slid off the runway, over a ditch, and into a cane field bordering the air strip. [46]

---

43 Landon received Silver Star and retired as four star general in 1963 with two Distinguished Flying Crosses. He died at age 80 and is buried in USAF Academy Cemetery.

44 Shigekazu Shimazaki was killed in action in 1945.

45 Lieutenant Bellows, 50th Aero Squadron, was awarded the Distinguished Service Cross for extraordinary heroism in action near Saint-Mihiel, France where he was killed on 13 September 1918 while performing a reconnaissance mission.

46 Lieutenant Richards' plane was a total loss. Assigned to another B-17, Captain Richards, of

08:55: Nine aircraft of the 4th Fighter Unit attacked Bellows Field in waves of three planes each. Three pilots of the 44th Pursuit Squadron who were at Bellows for gunnery training attempted to take off in their P-40s. Missourian Lieutenant George Whiteman got the first P-40 airborne only to be attacked by six Mitsubishi Zeros and shot down in a ball of flame at the end of the runway. He was the first US aviator to die in the War.[47] Lieutenant Hans Christiansen had started to get into the cockpit of his plane when he was stuck in the back by enemy fire and fell – dead – at the feet of his mechanic.[48] Lieutenant Sam Bishop managed to get airborne but his plane was hit repeatedly and, after losing hydraulic pressure and engine coolant, Bishop was forced to ditch in the surf one-half mile off the end of the runway. He swam to safety. No more pilots attempted to take off.

The bedlam was further compounded by a 2000-gallon aviation fuel truck that was quickly set ablaze and was spewing jets of fire and billowing, rolling black smoke into darken the sky overhead. Casualties totaled two killed and six wounded.

Haleiwa Landing field

Haleiwa was a short, sandy strip originally used as an emergency landing field. By 1941, pilots were spending two-week rotations to practice simulated combat conditions. The field had no permanent structures forcing officers and men to bring their own tents and equipment.

Second Lieutenant George Welch and Lieutenant Kenneth Taylor, from the 47th Pursuit Squadron, had attended a Christmas dinner-dance in a Waikiki hotel before retiring to an all-night poker game with fellow pilots at Wheeler Field. When the surprise attack hit Wheeler, Welch phoned to Haleiwa Field to prepare their planes.

Lt George Welch and Lt Kenneth Taylor USAF

The pair came under enemy fire during a wild, 11-mile drive to Haleiwa, but arrived safely to find that ground crews had their P-40s ready for action.

The duo headed for Barbers Point based upon information from Interceptor Control. The easily identified locale was a convenient rendezvous point for the

---

Indianapolis, Indiana and his entire crew died on 8 September 1942 during an attack against Japanese convoys off Papua New Guinea. On the return trip, the aircraft was engaged by a number of Japanese fighters and shot down on Rendova Island, off New Guinea. The crash caused bombs onboard to explode. Not discovered until 1943, the crew's remains were returned to the United States after the war and reburied in a mass grave at Jefferson Barracks National Cemetery, St. Louis, Missouri.

47   Lieutenant George Allison Whiteman (frequently misspelled as Whitman), the eldest of ten children, enlisted in 1939. For his gallantry that day, he was posthumously awarded the Silver Star. In 1955, Whiteman Air Force Base was renamed in his honor.

48   Second Lieutenant Hans Christiansen is buried at the National Cemetery of the Pacific.

attacking air fleet. Although the skies were empty of enemy planes, they observed twelve dive bombers punishing nearby Ewa Field. Welch shot down an enemy dive bomber with one burst from his three .30-caliber wing guns. While engaged in combat his plane was hit by an incendiary bullet which passed through the baggage compartment just in the rear of his seat. At this point he discovered that one gun was jammed. He climbed above the clouds, checked his plane, returned to Barbers Point, and immediately attacked a Japanese plane running out to sea, which he shot down with the plane falling into the ocean. Meanwhile Taylor shot down two planes. The pair flew to Wheeler Field to refuel and add .50-caliber ammunition to their cowling guns. By this time the First Wave attack was over.

Welch, Taylor and three other pilots took off to intercept second-wave fighters from the *Soryu* heading for Wheeler. Taylor drove headlong into six or eight Zeros. A neat turn and he was in their line. Welch shot down one, which was pouring bullets into Taylor's plane while Taylor was downing the enemy plane to his front. During this combat Welch's plane was struck by three bullets from the rear gun of the ship he was attacking; one striking his motor, one the propeller and one the cowling.

Taylor was wounded and landed. Welch found another dive bomber proceeding seaward, which he pursued and shot down about five miles off shore. Taylor and Welch accounted for seven of the eleven planes shot down by the five pilots. [49]

USS *Nevada*

Launched in 1914, USS *Nevada* was a leap forward in dreadnought technology because four new features that would be included on almost every subsequent US battleship: triple gun turrets, oil in place of coal for fuel, geared steam turbines for greater range, and heavy armor only in critical areas. These features made *Nevada* and its sister ship *Oklahoma*, the first US Navy super-dreadnoughts.

08:01: When the torpedo bombers of the first wave passed over the USS *Nevada*, Ensign Joseph Taussig, Officer of the Deck, repeatedly shouted over the PA system 'ALL HANDS, GENERAL QUARTERS. AIR RAID. THIS IS NO DRILL.' Machine-gunners aboard the Nevada hit an approaching torpedo bomber and it wobbled before plowing into the water. But the torpedo had been launched and it struck the port bow moments later. Taussig was rushing to his post as gunnery officer for the starboard antiaircraft batteries when a bomb fragment passed through his left hip and threw Taussig to the deck. Taussig found his shattered left leg tucked up under his arm, but he remained at his post. Chief Boatswain Edwin Hill led the effort to release the ship from her moorings. He dove off the ship to cast off the lines and swam back to assume his duties on

49   Both Welch and Taylor were awarded Distinguished Service Crosses.
Born George Louis Schwartz, Jr., his changed his name due to anti-German sentiments during the First World War. Lieutenant George Schwartz Welch had completed three years of a mechanical engineering degree from Purdue University before joining the Army Air Corps in 1939. Welch flew a total of 348 combat missions during the war with sixteen confirmed victories before malaria forced his retirement. After the war Welch became a test pilot until in 1954 his F-100 Super Sabre disintegrated during a 7g pullout at Mach 1.55. He is buried in Arlington National Cemetery.
Lieutenant Kenneth Marlar Taylor was born in Enid, Oklahoma. He joined the military after two years at the University of Oklahoma. After flying in the Pacific in World War II, Taylor retired as an Air Force brigadier general and died in Tucson in 2006 at age 86.

board, but he was killed when a bomb struck the bow. [50]

08:40: The USS *Nevada* cast off to escape the harbor as the Japanese Second Wave arrived. The process of getting a ship underway usually took 2 ½ hours to get up steam, four tugs to maneuver away from moorings, and an experienced captain to give orders, but the *Nevada* had none of that. What it did have was a middle-aged naval reservist, Lieutenant Commander Francis Thomas. With seventeen-year veteran Chief Quartermaster Robert Sedberry piloting, Thomas guided the ship past the searing heat of the burning *Arizona*, the sunken *West Virginia*, and capsized *Oklahoma* while 21 Aichi bombers from carrier *Kaga* swarmed the *Nevada* to sink it in the harbor mouth – a cork in the bottle that would trap ships in the harbor for months. Ten or fifteen bombs straddled the *Nevada* before the Japanese pilots found the range. Six bombs struck the forecastle forward of #1 turret and two bombs hit aft the stack. Another on the starboard side killed an entire gun crew as injured Ensign Taussig lay on a stretcher with his hopelessly shattered leg. [51]

09:10: With the ship's deck aflame and Thomas fearful of it being sunk in the narrow channel, Sedberry aimed for a spit of land known locally as Hospital Point. More bombs struck. Two tugs helped nose the ship out of the channel. The anchor dropped and the battleship grounded.[52]

All the fires were extinguished by 15:30. Twenty-nine *Nevada* sailors were dead, but remarkably all six Patten brothers from Odebolt, Iowa, who served in the *Nevada*'s engine room, survived.

USS *Pennsylvania* and the End of the Attack

The USS *Pennsylvania* was undergoing routine maintenance in the service area of Pearl Harbor. Because the Japanese attack initially focused on ships moored around Ford Island, the *Pennsylvania*'s guns were some of the first to return fire that morning.

09:07: Nine dive bombers from the carrier *Akagi* fell upon the dry-docked USS *Pennsylvania*. One bomb hit the battlewagon killing a starboard gun crew, but damage was minimal. Other bombs fell long in the same dock hitting destroyers USS *Cassin* and USS *Downes* causing uncontrollable fires. Efforts to extinguish the blaze by flooding the dry dock were defeated when the burning oil rose with the water level.

---

50   Boatswain Edwin Joseph Hill was born 1895 in Philadelphia and enlisted in the US Navy in 1912. Hill received the Medal of Honor posthumously for his actions during the attack and is buried in the National Cemetery of the Pacific.

51   Ensign Joseph K Taussig Jr was the son of a retired rear admiral. Taussig Sr had been reprimanded for testifying to a joint congressional committee that war with Japan was inevitable. Taussig Jr received a Navy Cross for his courageous action at Pearl Harbor but lost his leg after over four years in hospitals. After the amputation, he returned to active duty until retired in 1954. As a civilian, he returned to the Pentagon as deputy assistant secretary of the Navy. An Annapolis resident and third-generation Naval Academy graduate, Captain Taussig died in 1999 at age 79.

52   Lieutenant Commander Francis Thomas was awarded a Navy Cross for saving the endangered warship. He once joked, 'I'm the only officer ever to be awarded the Navy Cross for running a ship aground.' After Thomas retired as a rear admiral, he and his wife joined the Peace Corps. He died in 2005 at age 100.

Rescue efforts began almost immediately

Harbor craft rescue sailors while a fireboat pours water on the flaming USS *West Virginia. NARA*

Crewmen abandon the crippled USS *California* as the burning harbor oil approaches to eventually engulf the ship. NARA

Aerial view of Battleship Row on 10 December reveals a trail of oil from the sunken USS *Arizona*. The upturned USS *Oklahoma* is clearly visible. USS *California* lies surrounded by smaller craft in the upper left. NARA

The damage to American battleships was extensive, but only the *Arizona*, and *Oklahoma* never returned to combat

The crumpled remains of USS *Arizona* show the utter devatration of the Japanese attack. NARA

USS *Pennsylvania* in its drydock with the burnt hulk of the USS *Downes* and the capsized USS *Cassin* in front of the battle wagon. New ships also named *Downes* and *Cassin* were built from salvagable components. NARA

Capsized USS *Oklahoma* rests in the harbor mud while a rescue barge ties alongside. NARA

The *Pennsylvania* suffered fifteen dead, thirty-eight wounded, and fourteen missing.

09:12: The destroyer USS *Shaw* was in a separate dry dock slightly to the east. The Japanese planes attacking the dry dock hit the *Shaw* with three armor-piercing bombs. Naval sources speculate that the ship's forward fuel tanks ruptured spreading the flames through the ship. The order to abandon was given.

09:30: The *Shaw*'s forward magazine exploded in an incredible fireball that blew the bow from the rest of the hull. Twenty-four crewmen were killed.[53]

09:37: The magazines and torpedo warheads on the *Cassin* and *Downes* exploded and the vessels were abandoned. The USS *Cassin* rolled over onto the USS *Downes*.

09:45: The last Japanese plane left the skies over Oahu. In less than two hours the entire attack was over and the US Pacific Fleet was destroyed.

10:00: Commander Fuchida landed upon the violently tossing deck of the *Akagi*, the last plane to return to the carriers. Fuchida begged the admirals to launch another attack focused upon the oil storage tanks. However, without surprise and assuming that American planes were searching the ocean for his fleet, Admiral Nagumo thought the risk too great.

11:45: General Marshall's warning telegram was delivered to Fort Shafter, but it was not decoded until almost 15:00 – seven hours too late. A copy was then forwarded to Admiral Kimmel. After reading the warning, he furiously threw it into his wastebasket.

Midget Submarines (Part 2)

The Japanese midget submarine commanded by Ensign Kazuo Sakamaki developed a faulty compass but nevertheless he attempted to complete his mission with dead reckoning navigation. Sakamaki surfaced frequently to get bearings and joyfully witnessed the column of black smoke rising into the sky.

Japanese midget submarine beached NARA

08:17: The destroyer USS *Helm* steamed through the harbor neck in the bright morning sunshine. Its crew spotted the conning tower of a submarine on the vessel's starboard side of the entrance channel. Sakamaki's midget submarine had submerged only to bottom

---

53   Efforts to contain the fire aboard the *Shaw* were successful and unbelievably the repaired ship was seaworthy by February 1942.

on a reef. While the *Helm* fired its deck gun, the sub slipped over the reef and escaped.

Sakamaki, with his vessel's gyroscope inoperative, struck the reef three times while attempting to enter the harbor. The sub's violent motion temporarily knocked Sakamaki unconscious and batteries leaked filling the sub with white smoke. Sakamaki agonizingly shifted ballast and the sub slid off the coral, but without navigation aids the midget eventually grounded in Waimanlo Bay on the eastern shore of Oahu on 8 December. Sakamaki set demolition charges which failed to go off then swam ashore to become the first Japanese POW when he was captured by Hawaiian National Guard Corporal David Akui. [54]

08:39: Another of the midget submarines successfully entered the harbor and wildly launched its two torpedoes. One exploded upon hitting a dock and the second ran ashore. The destroyer USS *Monaghan* rammed and depth charged the midget. The vessel was recovered days later with the remains of its crew still on board.

09:50: The destroyer USS *Blue* under command of Navy Reservist Ensign Nathan F Asher detected a submarine approximately 5 miles south of Diamond Head and dropped six depth charges. A rising oil slick and air bubbles confirmed destruction of the enemy vessel. [55]

10:04: The USS *St Louis* steamed out of the harbor channel only to be attacked by two submarine launched torpedoes. To avoid an almost sure sinking, Captain George Rood ordered 'Emergency Full' and the ship left the harbor at 25 knots. Both torpedoes missed instead striking a reef near the harbor entrance. The *St Louis* fired its 5-inch deck gun upon the midget's conning tower, the gunners believing they scored hits. The nearby USS *Blue* dropped depth charges and observed an oil slick. Ensign Asher presumed a second submarine sank. [56]

Analysis

Although brilliantly conceived and executed, the Japanese attack presented some very notable failures. Japanese planes failed to locate and destroy the American aircraft carriers with disastrous consequences for the Japanese Navy only six months

---

54   Ensign Kazuo Sakamaki demanded to be allowed to commit suicide after his capture. Transferred to the United States, he was held at Camp McCoy, Wisconsin. After the war, Sakamaki became an ardent pacifist and worked with the Toyota Motor Corporation, becoming president of its Brazilian subsidiary. He died in 1999 at age 81.

Sakamaki's petty officer drowned while attempting to swim ashore. The midget submarine was salvaged and sent on a tour of the United States to encourage the purchase of War Bonds.

David Akui served through the remainder of the war in the Pacific Theater and was a member of the famed 'Merrill's Marauders', who fought the Japanese in the jungles of Burma. He survived the war to return to Oahu.

55   This midget submarine was recovered in 1960 from the Keehi Lagoon between Pearl Harbor and Honolulu. Although the location does not match Ensign Asher's report, the crippled vessel could have drifted toward the lagoon. In any case, the restored sub is on display at the Japanese Naval Academy.

56   The wreckage of the final sub was discovered inside Pearl Harbor in 1944 during removal operations of US ships destroyed in an accidental explosion. Wartime secrecy and haphazard disposal of the wreckage has led to ongoing speculation about this vessel's actions on 7 December. Possibly, midget sub #5 did fire its two torpedoes at the USS *West Virginia* and USS *Oklahoma*.

later when four Japanese carriers and a heavy cruiser were sunk during the Battle of Midway; they also failed to destroy the repair facilities allowing rapid repair of salvageable American ships; senior Japanese Navy commanders had little respect for submarines so they chose not to attack the US submarine base, as a consequence American submarines launched a devastating attack upon Japanese shipping for the remainder of the war; and they chose not to attack the oil storage tanks, bombing them would have delayed any American response until fuel reserves could be reestablished and would have sent 4.5 million gallons of flaming oil down the hillside onto American hospital facilities. The greatest mistake was the political decision to bring the United States into the war.

There were obviously damaging American failures as well. Despite the War Department's warning of 27 November that war was imminent, Admiral Kimmel's ships maintained only one lit boiler dramatically extending the time required to make way; ship and shore naval batteries were not continuously manned with ammunition at the ready; most of the senior officers lived ashore and were not

Admiral Chester Nimitz aboard USS Enterprise to present awards, 27 May 1942. Note capsized USS Oklahoma and sunken USS West Virginia and USS Arizona in the background NARA

on their ships when the attackers struck; no torpedo nets defended the ships; and the naval long range reconnaissance flights (700-to-800-mile radius) called for in the war plans were not performed. General Short had not ordered barrage balloons floated above the airfields nor a blackout of military and civilian areas; antiaircraft ammunition was stored in locked bunkers rather than distributed among the gun positions, which were not manned; and the short range (100-mile radius) reconnaissance flights, which were the army's responsibility, were not conducted. Technology failed as well – the primitive radar could not distinguish friend from foe. Worst of all, poor communications resulted in the Army not telling the Navy about the Opana radar tracks, thus the Navy's carrier aircraft lost the opportunity to locate and attack Nagumo's fleet.

Aftermath

The initial American response was disbelief. Army personnel wondered why the darn-fool Navy was running a drill on Sunday morning. Naval personnel wondered why the darn-fool Army was conducting a drill over the naval base. When the first black objects fell from the planes, both wondered what darn-fool pilot had accidentally released a bomb. Civilian and military living farther from Pearl Harbor who witnessed the attack applauded it as the most realistic drill ever. Author Edger Rice Burroughs, creator of Tarzan, was so unconcerned by the noise that he went to breakfast in his Honolulu hotel then played tennis.

Small boats zigzagged through the burning oil that covered the waters around Battleship Row picking up wounded or badly burned sailors who had jumped from the stricken ships. Many were completely naked having had their clothes literally blown off in the explosions. Sailors attempting to swim clear of the approaching wave of burning oil were strafed by Japanese fighters. The oil slick at Ford Island burned for 2 ½ days.

Off-base officers rushed to their posts – frequently with partial uniforms thrown over their pajamas. Traumatic shock was rampant. Even experienced officers wandered aimlessly in search of their commands.

A Ford Island Marine picked up a Japanese girl wandering about in confusion. Despite her repeated denials, 'I maid; no spy' the Marine chained her to a nearby eucalyptus tree. It was to be the start of a shameful suspicion of all Americans of Japanese descent.

In central Honolulu, 24-year-old professional boxer Toy Tamanaha and friends stopped to buy popsicles when an errant American antiaircraft shell blew up the store. Tamanaha woke up in the hospital with both legs amputated.[57]

Patriotism ran strong among all of the island's population. A call for blood donors brought 500 civilians to Queen's hospital in Honolulu. They calmly stood in line for hours. When the hospital ran out of blood bags, nurses stored the excess in sterilized Coca Cola bottles.

At Hickam, one hundred civilian employees arrived to assist fire fighting. Later in the afternoon at Schofield Barracks they hastily buried approximately four hundred dead.

The Ramsey family lived on Ford Island. After the bombs started to fall, 16-year-old Mary Ann Ramsey, daughter of Commander Logan Ramsey sheltered with her mother in Battery Henry Adair, an abandoned First World War concrete coastal gun battery under their home near Battleship Row. Soon vehicles of all types started arriving to deliver wounded from the *Arizona* to the shelter. Mary Ann recalled:

> A young man, filthy black oil covering his burned, shredded flesh, walked in unaided. The skin hung from his arms like scarlet ribbons as he staggered toward my mother for help. Looking at me, he gestured to his throat trying to speak; he must have swallowed some of the burning oil as he swam through the inferno. His light blue eyes against the whites, made

---

57   Tamanaha survived his injuries, married, and raised four daughters. In 1947 he was granted compensation by the US government for his injuries and opened a local store. Tamanaha died in Pearl City, Oahu, in July 1984.

more so by the oil clinging to his face, were luminous in visible shock at what they had seen and experienced that awful morning. We directed him to the mattresses now lining the corridor of the shelter, as the Marines herded us into a side room in order to keep the passageway clear for the arrival of more wounded.

Later in the day, Miss Ramsey circulated among patients on patio of the Marine Barracks where those beyond help had been placed. The 16-year-old held patient after patient in her arms until they died. She covered each with a blanket before moving on to the next.[58]

A skinny, 17-year-old American private missed his University of Hawaii class picnic date with a local Japanese girl. They had met while attending a special creative writing class. Ten years later James Jones penned *From Here to Eternity* based upon his experiences based on hawaii before the war.

False rumors abounded: planes returned for a third wave attack; paratroopers were sighted on the north coast; an invasion fleet was offshore; the water source for the island had been poisoned; a fifth column committed acts of sabotage; San Francisco was under attack. Trigger-happy soldiers and sailors fired at anything – and nothing, while terrified civilians huddled in blackout darkness.

General Short asked the territorial governor to declare martial law to head off any potential internal security problems. After consulting with President Roosevelt by phone, the governor agreed. It would remain in effect for the next three years. Meanwhile, FBI and local law enforcement quickly seized Japanese consular officials and 1,441 Japanese descendants and interned them on Sand Island located off Honolulu.

Six fighters from the *Enterprise* were sent to Ford Island that night with their landing lights on. While approaching over the *Pennsylvania*, first one, then another, then the entire fleet's antiaircraft guns opened fire. Five of the American fighters were shot down and three pilots killed and three sailors in the harbor were wounded by stray bullets. Why would attacking Japanese planes have their lights on?

Washington DC

13:47: Meanwhile, back in Washington, Secretary of War Frank Knox was about to lunch when Chief of Naval Operations Admiral Harold Stark reported a message from Hawaii: WE ARE BEING ATTACKED. THIS IS NO DRILL - from CINC Pacific. Knox, focused upon Southeast Asia, at first thought it meant the Philippines. Three minutes later he informed President Roosevelt. Impossible FDR thought.

14:05: After the Japanese planes had started their attack, Ambassador Nomura arrived at the State Department to deliver the 14-part message.

14:20: Nomura was led into Secretary of State Hull's office. Hull, already aware of the contents of the message, did not shake Nomura's hand or even offer the ambassador a chair. The 14th part stated:

The Japanese government regrets to have to notify hereby the American

---

58   Mary Ann Ramsey became a free-lance writer specializing in health care, an editor-writer for a Philadelphia magazine, and later director of public relations for several area medical centers including The Children's Hospital of Philadelphia. She died in 2004 at age 79.

Government that in view of the attitude of the American Government it cannot but consider that it is impossible to reach an agreement through further negotiations.

Hull's chilling reply reflected his contempt:

In all my fifty years of public service I have never seen a document that was more crowded with infamous falsehoods and distortions … on a scale so huge that I never imagined until today that any Government on this planet was capable of uttering them.

Hull raised his hand to stifle any protest and nodded towards the door. [59]

14:37: President Roosevelt's press secretary telephoned the wire services to announce the attack to the nation.

In response to the news, a patriot chopped down four Japanese cherry trees in the Tidal Basin. In another part of Washington, 27,000 people watched Sammy Baugh throw two fourth quarter touchdown passes to pull out a Washington Redskins defeat of the Philadelphia Eagles 20-14. It was the last game of the season. In attendance was a young naval ensign – John F Kennedy. In the press box, the AP sports writer received a message from his office: 'Japs just kicked off. War now.' Meanwhile Brigadier General Dwight Eisenhower, just off maneuvers in San Antonio, Texas, got the call from his commander to report and told his wife Mamie 'I have to go to headquarters. I don't know when I'll be back.' The absence would be four years.

The next day President Roosevelt began his speech to the Joint Session of Congress:

Yesterday, December 7, 1941 – a date which will live in infamy – the

President Roosevelt presents his speech before congress NARA

59   Secretary of State Cordell Hull was awarded the Nobel Peace Prize in 1945 for his role in creating the founding documents and principles of the United Nations.

United States of America was suddenly and deliberately attacked by naval and air forces of the Empire of Japan.

By 13:00 on 8 December, the vote was 82-0 in the Senate and 388-1 in the House.[60] The United States had entered the Second World War.

The Japanese successfully struck American, Dutch, and British installations. The invasion of Malaya proceeded that morning as planned. At 04:00 local time (8 December, but still 7 December in Hawaii), bombs fell upon Singapore. At 12:35 in the Philippines Japanese bombers appeared over the B-17s parked on unalerted Clark Field. Guam fell after a brief struggle on 12 December; Wake Island on 23 December; and Hong Kong on Christmas Day.

Guilt and Retribution

The Roberts Commission, chaired by Supreme Court Justice Owen Roberts, was established to ascertain blame for the debacle. It found Kimmel and Short guilty of errors of judgment and dereliction of duty. Kimmel argued that important information had been withheld from him. Short said that he was in command and therefore responsible.[61]

Nonetheless, General Short was demoted two ranks and forcibly retired as a major general in February 1942. He worked for Ford Motor Company in Dallas before dying in 1949.

Admiral Kimmel was also reduced to two-star rank and retired in early 1942. Admiral Kimmel's grief did not end there. Kimmel had three sons, all of whom served in the war. Manning Kimmel commanded a submarine that was sunk in July 1944. The Japanese captured a few survivors including Manning. They pushed them into a ditch, doused them with gasoline, and lit them. Admiral Kimmel died in 1968 at age 86.

In 1944, the Army Pearl Harbor Board censured Army Chief of Staff George Marshal and War Plans chief General Leonard Gerow for not keeping Short fully informed of the collapsing diplomatic situation with Japan. A Navy Board of Inquiry also criticized Chief of Naval Operations Harold Stark for inadequately warning Kimmel. [62]

Legend has it that Admiral Yamamoto, upon hearing that the diplomatic note arrived after the Pearl Harbor attack had started, said, 'I fear all we have done today is to awaken a great sleeping giant and fill him with a terrible resolve.' On 18 April 1943, Yamamoto left Rabual, Solomon Islands to inspect Japanese airfields. The coded message describing his trip was intercepted and broken by American decoders

---

60   Jeannette Rankin from Montana, a women's rights campaigner, pacifist, and the first woman elected to Congress, cast the only no vote. When pressured to at least abstain, Rankin stated, 'As a woman, I can't go to war and I refuse to send anyone else.' She had also cast a no vote against the United States entering the First World War in 1917. The vote cost her political career and she did not run for re-election.

61   Historians and politicians continue to argue over Kimmel's and Short's culpability. In 1999 the United States Senate passed a non-binding resolution to exonerate Kimmel and Short. Presidents Clinton, Bush, and Obama refused to approve the resolution.

62   Stark was demoted and transferred to London as commander of US Naval Forces – Europe. General Douglas MacArthur, whose negligence in the Philippines was even more grievous, escaped censure.

at Pearl Harbor. Admiral Nimitz, then CINC Pacific, approved a squadron of eighteen P-38s Lightnings from Guadalcanal to intercept. The admiral's Mitsubishi transport and all nine accompanying Zeros were shot down. The admiral's body was found in the New Guinea jungle the next day.

Last known image of Admiral Yamamota.

Admiral Nagumo was shattered by the loss of four carriers during the Battle of Midway and contemplated suicide. He eventually did commit suicide in July 1944 after devastating losses during the Battle of the Philippine Sea. Commander Fuchida had a brilliant wartime career. On 19 February 1942, he led his squadron in an attack upon Darwin, Australia that destroyed planes, ships, and so devastated the city that it was abandoned. Forty-five days later he led the attack upon British naval vessels in Colombo, Ceylon sinking an aircraft carrier, destroyer, and two cruisers. Fuchida broke both legs abandoning the sinking *Akagi* during the Battle of Midway. His long convalescence ended in 1944 only to experience the destruction of the Japanese Combined Fleet and the death of many of his comrades at the Battle of the Philippine Sea on 20 April 1944.

After the war, Fuchida read a pamphlet on forgiveness written by Jacob DeShazer, a bombardier in the 1942 Doolittle Raid on Tokyo. DeShazer had been captured, imprisoned and tortured by the Japanese. The American had found God through his experiences and converted Fuchida to Christianity. Fuchida, the man who led the surprise attack, became a Presbyterian evangelist and settled in Seattle, Washington. He died in 1976 at age 73.

What happened to the battleships? The shipyard engineers and salvage crews worked miracles in recovering the damaged ships. By 20 December, the *Pennsylvania*, *Tennessee*, and *Maryland* were back in service. The *California* was operational by the end of 1943. The *West Virginia* was raised and refitted by July 1944. All five recovered battleships got their revenge with the utter annihilation of the remaining Japanese fleet during the Battle of Leyte Gulf in October 1944 where Japanese losses included four carriers, three battleships, nine cruisers, eight destroyers, and 65,000 men. The *Nevada* was operational by the end of 1942 and participated in the D-Day invasion of Normandy, France. The *West Virginia* joined 260 other Allied ships in Tokyo Bay for the Japanese surrender. The by-then obsolete USS *Oklahoma* was raised but it later sank in a Pacific storm on its way to a West Coast scrap yard in the spring of 1947. In reality, the disaster at Pearl Harbor marked the end of the battleship era.

Casualties

The Pearl Harbor attack was the worst defeat in American Naval history. Altogether, 2,403 were killed and 1,178 wounded; 188 aircraft destroyed, 151 aircraft damaged, and 18 ships sunk or severely damaged including all eight battleships, three cruisers, and four destroyers. Sixty percent of the injuries were second and third degree burns. Included among the dead were sixty-eight civilians, most after being hit by spent or improperly fused antiaircraft shells.

Japanese losses were slight: twenty-nine planes, five midget submarines, one I-class submarine, forty-five airmen, 121 submarine crewmen, and nine midget submarine crewmen. One POW taken.

America would forever more 'Remember Pearl Harbor.'

Battlefield Tour

British explorer James Cook arrived in the Hawaiian Islands in 1778. Within five years, European military technology helped King Kamehameha I conquer and unify the islands and establish the Kingdom of Hawaii as an attractive commercial location due to its sugar industry and the whaling trade.

A peaceful revolution supported by American sailors and Marines overthrew the Hawaiian monarchy of Queen Liliuokalani in 1893. The short-lived Republic of Hawaii was formed followed by formal annexation by the United States in 1898. American expansion in the Pacific led to creation of Naval Station Pearl Harbor in 1908. Although temporarily halted by the Great Depression, expansion of the facilities resumed in reaction to Japanese aggression in the late 1930s. The newly-created United States Pacific Fleet relocated to Hawaii in February 1941. [63]

Oahu bristles with military sites – some abandoned; some immortalized; and some still engaged in military activity. Obviously, activity intensified after 7 December to the point that the island became known as the 'Gibraltar of the Pacific.' By the end of the war, it was the most heavily fortified island in the world.

Pearl Harbor, Ford Island, Hickam Field, Wheeler Field, and Kaneohe Bay Air Station continue to serve as active military bases; therefore, access is limited to those with military identification.

Pearl Harbor
World War II Valor in the Pacific National Monument
Visitor Center Address: 1 Arizona Memorial Place, Honolulu, HI 96818
Mailing Address: 1845 Wasp Blvd, Bldg #176, Honolulu HI 96818
Tel: 808-422-3399
Web: https://www.nps.gov/valr/index.htm

Open daily from 07:00 to 17:00. There are several free parking lots at the visitor center. The *Arizona* and Ford Island are visitable by non-military guests, but access is tightly controlled and packages and purses are not allowed. We recommend purchase of the Passport to Pearl Harbor which permits visits to all of the Pearl Harbor sites. The grounds are fully accessible to visitors in wheelchairs. (21.367276, -157.938066)

There are four main sites at the WWII Valor in the Pacific National Monument. The USS *Arizona* Memorial, jointly operated by the National Park Service and the US Navy; the USS *Bowfin* Submarine Museum and Park; the battleship USS *Missouri* Memorial; and the Pacific Aviation Museum Pearl Harbor. Each is described in more detail below.

USS *Arizona* Memorial
Reservations: 877-444-6777
Web: http://www.pearlharborhistoricsites.org/pearl-harbor/arizona-memorial

---

63   Admiral James Otto Richardson, Pacific Fleet commander, protested against the redeployment of the Pacific Fleet from San Diego to Pearl Harbor believing it became vulnerable to air and torpedo attacks and that the Pacific Fleet would be the logical first target in the event of war with Japan. He was relieved of his command.

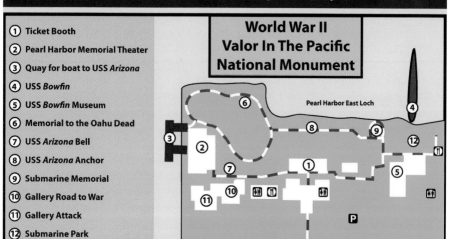

Valor in the Pacific sites (on shore)

1. Ticket Booth
2. Pearl Harbor Memorial Theater
3. Quay for boat to USS *Arizona*
4. USS *Bowfin*
5. USS *Bowfin* Museum
6. Memorial to the Oahu Dead
7. USS *Arizona* Bell
8. USS *Arizona* Anchor
9. Submarine Memorial
10. Gallery Road to War
11. Gallery Attack
12. Submarine Park

World War II Valor In The Pacific National Monument

Pearl Harbor East Loch

Submarine Memorial, (left).

USS *Bowfin* 5-in deck gun, (right).

USS *Bowfin* lies in front of the Ford Island Bridge, below).

The Arizona Memorial stands in tribute to the 1,177 sailors and marines who died as a result of the attack

The *Arizona* Memorial and the sunken s ship's mooring piers.

Gun turret #3 rises above the water's surface, (above) and is visible behind the flag pole when viewed through one of the memorial's seven windows. The flag pole was the earliest commemoration of the *Arizona* and was attached to its mast in 1950, (right).

The USS *Arizona* Memorial Program includes a 23-minute documentary followed by the US Navy boat ride to the memorial, time at the memorial, and the boat ride back. All together, the USS *Arizona* Memorial program lasts 1 hour and 15 minutes. It is highly recommended that the free, timed tickets be obtained in advance even though the National Park Service gives out 1,300 walk-in tickets daily, on a first come, first served basis. The first USS *Arizona* Memorial movie/boat program begins at 07:30 and runs every 15 minutes until 15:00. The memorial receives over one million visitors each year. Open daily except Thanksgiving, Christmas, and New Year's Day. No admission charge. (21.364875, -157.949981)

By the end of 1943, most of the ship above the waterline had been removed. Among the reuseable items were guns, ammunition, machinery, the stern aircraft crane, conning tower, and numerous other components. The US Army removed gun turrets #3 and #4 and the triple 14-inch guns were installed as shore batteries at Kahe Point (Battery Arizona) and Mokapu Point. They have been dismantled and remain in a scrap yard on Ford Island.

The USS *Arizona* Memorial, designed by Austrian-born architect Alfred Preis, was built in 1962 and spans the ship's beam without touching the sunken battleship. The sweep of the broad white marble cenotaph symbolizes initial defeat, agonizing recovery, and ultimate victory. The Assembly Hall symbolically presents seven windows on each side representative of the day of the attack. The marble Shrine at the far end inscribes the names of all of the crewmen who lost their lives. A hole in the floor permits viewing the wreckage below. The circular base of gun turret #3 is sometimes visible above the water level.

The ship's bunkers continue to leak oil at the rate of about nine quarts per day. The oil slick on the water's surface is referred to by some as the *Arizona*'s tears. Those who served on the ship on 7 December are offered the privilege of having their ashes placed in underwater turret #4 by navy divers.

USS *Bowfin* Submarine Museum & Park
11 Arizona Memorial Drive, Honolulu, Hawaii 96818-3104
Tel: 808-423-1341
Web: http://www.bowfin.org
Email: info@bowfin.org
Open daily from 07:00 to 17:00. (21.368752, -157.939418)

USS *Bowfin* (SS-287), a fleet attack submarine, was launched on 7 December 1942 in the Portsmouth Navy Yard in Maine and fought in the Pacific. The *Bowfin* completed nine war patrols earning a Presidential Unit Citation for its second patrol after sinking five large vessels and eight smaller craft. During the course of the entire war, *Bowfin* received official credit for sinking 16 large vessels and 22 small craft.

In 1979 a non-profit organization received ownership of the *Bowfin* for the purpose of establishing it as a memorial and museum to the submariners of the Second World War. After extensive restoration, the ship was moved to its current position the following year. The surface decks and central passageway of the submarine may be toured as well as a museum housing numerous Bowfin artifacts.

Submarine Park includes a Waterfront Memorial dedicated to the fifty-two submarines and more than 3,500 officers and crewmen lost during the Second World War. This memorial honors their enduring memory by telling the story of each lost vessel. (21.368309, -157.939028) The park also holds the conning tower from the USS *Parche* which may be entered to view the operational center of a WW II submarine. (21.368959, -157.938664) A Japanese

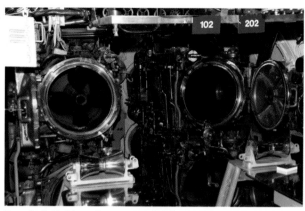

Loaded (left) and empty (right) torpedo tubes in the USS *Bowfin*

Kaiten one-man suicide torpedo is also on display. (21.368980, -157.938511)

To the south near the theater, the circular **Memorial to the Oahu Dead**, which looks across the loch at the *Arizona* Memorial, lists the names of all killed on each ship struck during the attack. (21.367151, -157.939606)

Ford Island

Ford Island is accessible by civilian personnel only via shuttle buses which depart every 15 minutes from the Pearl Harbor Visitors Center from 08:00 to 16:00 daily. For security reasons, no bags are allowed on the shuttle bus to Ford Island. Lockers are available near the ticket booth.

The Battleship *Missouri* Memorial

Tel: 877-644-4896

Web: https://ussmissouri.org

Open daily except Thanksgiving, Christmas, and New Year's Day. The Surrender Deck is handicap accessible, but above and below deck locations are not. Admission fee (21.362176, -157.953334)

The USS *Missouri* was launched on 29 January 1944 in the Brooklyn Navy Yard and it was the last battleship ever built by the US Navy. The ship's high cruising speed of 33 knots and nine 16-inch guns made it a formidable surface fleet weapon. The *Missouri* supported the land invasions of Iwo Jima and Okinawa and was proceeding to bombard the Japanese home islands when the surrender occurred. The Japanese formal surrender took place on its decks in Tokyo harbor on 2 September 1945 under the watchful eye of General Douglas MacArthur. Representatives of the Empire of Japan, but not the Emperor, signed two copies of the Instrument of Surrender. The Second World War officially ended as General MacArthur declared 'These proceedings are closed.'

The ship may be toured in a variety of ways depending upon one's interest and time available. Two 35-minute guided tours are offered each day and they are

Valor in the Pacific (Ford Island)

Ford Island Bridge

Ford Island

Ford Island Sites

① World War II Valor in the Pacific National Monument
② USS *Arizona*
③ USS *Missouri*
④ USS *Nevada* Mooring Quay
⑤ USS *Oklahoma* Memorial
⑥ Pacific Aviation Museum
⑦ USS *Utah* Memorial
⑧ USS *Nevada* Memorial

Ford island control tower as it appears today, above). Gun deck of the USS *Missouri*, (above right). Memorial to the 429 men who died aboard the USS *Oklahoma*, (left).

included in the Mighty Mo Pass - General Admission ticket. Alternatively, audio headphones are available for no extra charge for visitors to explore more than 100 locations above and below deck including the surrender deck where Admiral Perry's flag remains on display. Tour guides occupy key positions to offer explanations of the ship's functions. For an addition fee, the detailed and more strenuous Heart of the Missouri Tour is also

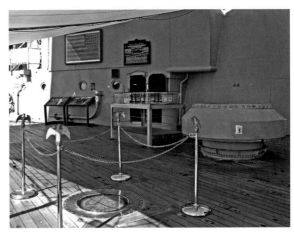

USS Missouri Surrender Deck

available which accesses areas generally not open including engine room and gun turrets.

USS *Oklahoma* Memorial

The *Oklahoma* Memorial remembers the 429 sailors and marines who were trapped inside the overturned ship's hull on 7 December. A black granite wall symbolizing the bow of a ship and bearing the image of the Oklahoma lists the names of the dead and frames 429 white standards representing sailors in formation. Each standard carries the name of one of the dead. The simple formation is located inland from the *Missouri* since that ship occupies what was the *Oklahoma*'s berth. (21.363509, -157.954412)

USS *Utah* Memorial

A simple brass plaque approached via a white concrete walkway is attached to the still overturned hull of the USS *Utah* on the western side of Ford Island. The decision was made in 1944 to leave the bodies of fifty-eight crewmen onboard, considering them buried at sea, thus the wreckage is considered a war grave. Since the base is restricted, it can be visited only by those with military identification. (21.368691, -157.961915)

USS *Nevada* Memorial

A memorial stone has been erected near the location on Hospital Point where the Nevada ran aground on what is now Joint Base Pearl Harbor - Hickam. The site is only accessible to those with military identification or civilians accompanied by a military sponsor. (21.350452, -157.966401)

Pacific Aviation Museum Pearl Harbor

319 Lexington Boulevard, Honolulu, Hawaii 96818
Tel: 808-441-1000
Web: https://www.pacificaviationmuseum.org

Open daily 08:00 to 17:00 except Thanksgiving, Christmas, and New Year's Day. In addition to the general admission, guided tours and flight simulators are available for an extra charge. (21.359842, -157.961840)

The 42,000-square-foot museum consists of Hangers 37 and 79 which hold a variety of Second World War and post-war aircraft. Hanger 37, with

Pacific Aviaion Museum Mitsubishi Zero

the assistance of an audio guide, allows an up close inspection of some of the war's famous aircraft including a Mitsubishi A6M2 Model 21 Type 0 'Zero' (fighter), North American B-25B 'Mitchell' (a medium bomber similar to one used in the Doolittle Raid on Japan in April 1942), Curtiss P-40 'Warhawk', Grumman F4F3 'Wildcat' (fighter), and a Douglas SBD 'Dauntless' (dive bomber). A 12-minute movie covers the surprise attack on Pearl Harbor and includes startling historic footage.

Hanger 79 is an original 1941 seaplane hangar whose older blue tint windows still display bullet holes from Japanese strafing. Now it holds jets and helicopters from later wars. Included are Korean War era Mikoyan-Gurevich MiG-15 and MiG-21 (fighters), North American Aviation F-86 'Sabre' (interceptor), Vietnam era Bell AH-1 'Cobra' (attack helicopter), and General Dynamics F-111C 'Aardvark' (fighter-bomber) among many other aircraft. In some instances, the craft may even be entered.

The **Ford Island Control Tower** stands outside the hanger. The brightly painted column is actually a water tank; the 1941 control room is the smaller white building on the low roof. The upper control tower atop the water tank was completed in 1942. (21.360708, -157.961527)

Environs of Honolulu
Fort Shafter

Fort Shafter was opened in 1907 as part of the War Department's ambitious construction program. The post was named after Major General William R Shafter, who led the US expedition to Cuba in 1898.

In 1941, the Hawaiian Department had its headquarters at Fort Shafter with an underground command post at the Red Hill ordnance depot in the Aliamanu Crater. Overall Army strength was 43,000 including Army Air Corps and Hawaiian National Guard units. The Hawaiian Coast Artillery Command had its headquarters at Fort Ruger and four coast artillery regiments stationed at Fort Armstrong, Fort Barrette, Fort Derussy, Diamond Head, Fort Kamehameha, Kuwaaohe Military Reservation (Fort Hase), and Fort Weaver.

Today Fort Shafter is headquarters for the United States Army Pacific Command. As an operating military base, the fort is open only to those with a military identification card and civilians accompanied by a military sponsor. A virtual tour of this historic installation is available at: http://www.usarpac.army.mil/tour00. asp. The itinerary starts at the fort's central plaza, Palm Circle, which is lined with administrative offices and commanding officers' homes including Quarters 5 once occupied by General Short. Plaques in Centennial Plaza provide a snapshot of the important role that the Army has played in the Pacific Theater giving a brief history of US Army involvement in the Spanish-American War (1898), the Boxer Rebellion in China (1900), the Philippine Insurrection (1899-1902), the Siberian Expedition (1918-1920), World War II (1941-1945), the Korean War (1950-1953), and the Vietnam War (1955-1975). Richardson Hall, the current United States Army Pacific Command headquarters building, displays two bronze panels at the entrance to the building containing the insignia of all divisions and units that trained and fought in the Pacific Theater in World War II. One panel also commemorates beloved journalist Ernie Pyle, killed while serving in the Pacific in April 1945. Inside, the mural 'Marching Men' depicts army personal training on Oahu.

The nearby gazebo marks the location of the original post headquarters building which burned down in 1982. The building housed the Roberts Commission hearings into the Pearl Harbor surprise attack.

Fort Derussy / U.S. Army Museum of Hawaii
2161 Kalia Rd, Honolulu, HI 96815
Web: http://www.hiarmymuseumsoc.org/index.html
Open Tuesday through Saturday from 10:00 until 17:00. Free; audio guides are available. Parking is located across the street at a discounted rate. (21.279068, -157.833792)

In 1906 a plan was developed to construct a system of coastal artillery batteries including Battery Randolph and Battery Dudley at Fort Derussy to protect Pearl Harbor and Honolulu. The former Randolph Battery houses the US Army Museum of Hawaii whereas Battery Dudley was demolished in 1970. Military vehicles line the front of the museum including a garishly-painted three-man Japanese light tank, a US M24 light tank, and a 105-mm M3 airborne howitzer. Museum exhibits displayed in the various shell, powder, and hoist rooms of the battery relate the early history of Hawaii, the establishment of American presence in the islands, Hawaiian military activities in the First and Second World Wars, Korea, and Vietnam. A Hall of Heroes honors Hawaiian recipients of the Medal of Honor and Distinguished Service Cross or its Navy equivalent, the Navy Cross. The battery's two 14 inch rifles were housed in retractable pits now sited incongruously near the Hotel Castle Waikiki Shore. The rooftop guns can be accessed from inside the museum.

Coastal Battery Gun at Fort Derussy

National Cemetery of the Pacific (Punchbowl or Puowaina)
2177 Puowaina Drive, Honolulu, HI 96813
Tel: 808-532-3720 / Fax: 808-532-3756
Web: https://www.cem.va.gov/cems/nchp/nmcp.asp
Open daily from 08:00 to 18:00. Free. (21.311735, -157.844982)

The 'Punchbowl' crater was formed some 75,000 to 100,000 years ago as a result of the ejection of hot lava through cracks in the old coral reefs. The site was used as an altar where Hawaiians offered human sacrifices to pagan gods and killed violators of their many taboos - thereby giving the crater its Hawaiian name *Puowaina*, most commonly translated as 'Hill of Sacrifice.' In the 1930s, the crater was used as a rifle range by the Hawaii National Guard. Toward the end of World War II, tunnels were dug through the rim of the crater for the placement of shore batteries to guard Honolulu Harbor and the south edge of Pearl Harbor.

Construction of the military cemetery began in 1948 with the first internments the following year with services for five war dead: an unknown serviceman, two Marines, an Army lieutenant and one civilian – noted war correspondent Ernie Pyle.[64] The cemetery still actively accepts the remains of military personnel and family members now holding over 34,000 graves of which 13,000 soldiers and sailors died during the Second World War. The cemetery recognizes thirty-three Medal of Honor recipients from America's wars whose graves are identified by gold lettering.[65]

The names of 28,788 military personnel who are missing in action or were lost or buried at sea in the Pacific are listed on marble slabs in ten Courts of the Missing which flank the Honolulu Memorial's grand stone staircase. At the top of the staircase in the Court of Honor, a statue of Lady Columbia, also known as Lady Liberty or Justice, stands on the bow of a ship holding a laurel branch representing all grieving mothers. The inscription below the statue, taken from a letter to Mrs Lydia Bixby, reads:[66]

> The solemn pride
> That must be yours
> To have laid
> So costly a sacrifice
> Upon the altar
> Of freedom
> - Abraham Lincoln

---

64   Seaman Third Class Ernest Taylor Pyle, a First World War veteran, was killed by a Japanese sniper on Ie Shima, an island off the northern coast of Okinawa on April 18, 1945.

65   Other notable burials include:
 Hawaii-born Colonel Ellison Shoji Onizuka was an aerospace engineer, flight test officer, and a member of space shuttle *Challenger* when it exploded on lift off on 28 January 1986. Col. Onizuka posthumously received the Congressional Space Medal of Honor in 2004, bestowed on individuals who perish during flight.
Daniel Inouye, a World War II Medal of Honor recipient, entered politics and became Hawaii's first post-statehood Representative (1959–1963) and longtime Senator (1963–2012).

66   Lydia Parker Bixby, a widow living in Boston, Massachusetts, was thought to have lost five sons in the Union Army during the American Civil War. President Abraham Lincoln wrote to Mrs Bixby to express the nation's sorrow at her loss.

A memorial pathway is lined with sixty memorials of varying design that have been donated by various organizations and foreign governments to honor America's veterans. Breathtaking views of the Island of Oahu may be found while standing at the highest point on the crater's rim. (21.310910, -157.848050) One of the gun pits established upon the Punchbowl crater remains visible. (21.310170, -157.847274)

> Exit the cemetery by following Puowaina Drive; turn right at the first opportunity onto what is also Puowaina Drive. Continue straight across the bridge and onto Tantalus Drive. (21.316201, -157.841730)

Tantalus Scenic Drive

A scenic drive through the hills above Honolulu and Waikiki is easily accessible from the National Cemetery of the Pacific. Follow Tantalus Drive for 4.6 miles as it clears the final houses and crosses over a ridge and into Makiki Valley. The road switchbacks up to travel along the top of the ridge then passes through forest where views are possible through breaks in the roadside trees. The road changes name to Round Top Drive after a hairpin turn to the left. (21.330039, -157.814277) Follow Round Top Drive for 2.5 miles to a turn to the right that accesses Tantalus Lookout for stunning views of the city, Punchbowl, and Diamond Head in the distance. (21.313855, -157.822445) Return to Round Top Drive and continue an additional 2.2 miles as the road drops in elevation to a viewpoint. (21.311031, -157.823209) The road re-enters a built-up area where it changes name several times before reaching Hawaiian Highway 1. Trailheads for three hiking routes that make up the Makiki Valley Loop are passed along the route. Contact local tourist or hiking organizations (or https://www.hikingproject.com) for details.

Fort Ruger

Fort Ruger, named after Civil War Major General Howard Ruger, was constructed as part of the 1906 plan to defend Honolulu and Pearl Harbor. The fort occupied most of Diamond Head crater and some surrounding territory originally holding four batteries positioned along the east slopes of Diamond Head and one on Kupikipiki'O Point. They were disarmed after the First World War. Two new batteries were constructed in the 1930s, but they never engaged the enemy. Construction of two casemates (Battery 407-Fort Ruger) on the south rim began after the war started, but they were never completed. Battery 155-Koko Head was completed and held 155-mm field guns. Much of Fort Ruger is still used by the Hawaiian Army National Guard.

Diamond Head State Monument

Diamond Head Rd, Honolulu, HI 96815
Tel: 800-464-2924

Open daily 06:00 to 18:00. Admission fee; limited parking; bring water, hat, and sunscreen and expect to take two hours for the round trip. (Trailhead: 21.263131, -157.804366)

Diamond Head is an extinct volcano that sits near the eastern end of Waikiki Beach. The height and distinctive outline of the caldera rim have made the volcano the trademark of Hawaii. The crater is entered through Kahala Tunnel. (21.263922, -157.800313)

Diamond Head's crater rim became a major Oahu defensive installation

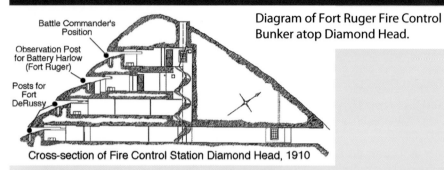

Diagram of Fort Ruger Fire Control Bunker atop Diamond Head.

Cross-section of Fire Control Station Diamond Head, 1910

Unused bunker of Battery 407 is visible from the Fire Control Center.

Spectacular views of Waikiki and Honolulu can be had from the Fire Control Center's rooftop. The low pink building along the beach is the famous Royal Hawaiian Hotel.

Diamond Head area historical monuments

Diamond Head light-
house as viewed from
the crater rim.

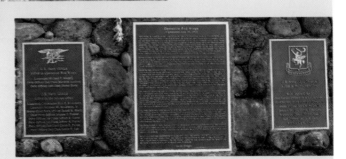

Operation Red Wings
Medal of Honor Memorial
(left) and plaques that
describe the mission,
(below).

Amelia Earhart Memorial
stone commemorating the
first solo transpacific flight
in 1934.

The **Diamond Head Summit Trail** starts across the level interior of the crater before the strenuous trail raises 560 feet over 0.8 miles. The switchbacks are often steep and uneven. Seventy-four steps, a 225-foot-long tunnel, and ninety-nine more steps followed by a three-story spiral stairway accesses the third of four levels of the Fort Ruger Fire Control Station that once directed the coastal batteries. The top-most level is blocked-off. Outside the fire control station, another fifty-four steps brings one to the 360-degree panoramic views of Honolulu, Waikiki, and the coastline that rewards visitors for their efforts. The two casemates from Battery 407 may be seen from the summit as well as operational military communications antennae.

Diamond Head lighthouse can be seen along the shoreline below along Diamond Head Road. Originally built in 1899 after two ships crashed on the nearby rocks, the fifty-five foot reinforced concrete tower now on the site was constructed in 1916. The grounds remain the home of the commander of the Fourteenth Coast Guard District. (21.255706, -157.809450)

Only one minute east of the lighthouse, a memorial stone marks the **Amelia Earhart Lookout**. Earhart became the first person to fly solo from Hawaii to the mainland after she left Wheeler Field in 1934 and arrived in Oakland, California 18 hours later. The site is now more popular for its views of the coastline than for its historical significance. (21.256053, -157.804870)

An open grassy area in Waialae-Kahala east of Diamond Head holds the **Operation Red Wings Medal of Honor Park**, which honors those who died during Operation Red Wings and all Hawaiian Medal of Honor recipients. The field stone memorial bears plaques listing the names of the Navy Seal members who were ambushed and cut-off and the men who died trying to rescue them on 28 June 2005. In that incident, a four-man Seal team stationed on Hawaii sought to capture a noted Taliban terrorist in Afghanistan. Lieutenant Michael Murphy sought exposed ground in the mountainous region to transmit a request for assistance. Lt Murphy died in the ensuing firefight. He was awarded a Medal of Honor for his sacrifice for his team. Three members of the four-man team including Lt Murphy were killed as were eight US Army Night Stalkers and eight US Navy Seals when a rescue helicopter was struck by a rocket propelled grenade. (21.259543, -157.795912)

Central Oahu

Leave the Honolulu / Pearl Harbor area west on highway H1; then north on highway H2 which becomes state route 99 (Wilikina Dr). After a short distance, turn left onto Kunia Rd. Entry requirements: military identification; for civilian access turn right at Lyman Rd to the Lyman Gate, which is the second entrance along Kunia Road (21.485044, -158.044800).

The guard will direct you to the Vehicle Processing Center. Everybody in the vehicle over the age of 16 must have valid photo identification; the vehicle operator must have a valid driver's license, motor vehicle registration, insurance, and safety check or rental car agreement. International visitors must be escorted by a Department of Defense cardholder.

Continue on Lyman Road for 0.3 miles; turn right on Flager Rd. Follow Flager (becomes Kolekole Ave) for 0.5 miles to enter a traffic circle that faces the museum. Take the 3rd exit, then immediately left to park.

Schofield Barracks

Schofield Barracks, originally part of the former Hawaiian Crown Lands, was ceded to the US government in 1899. Base construction was not started until nine years later and it was named after General John M Schofield, former commanding general of the US Army, who had originally identified its strategic value. The base has been home to the 25th Infantry Division since 1921.

Tropic Lightning Museum
Building 361, Kolekole and Waianae Ave, Schofield Barracks, HI 96857
Tel: 808-655-0438
Web: https://www.garrison. hawaii.army.mil/tlm/index. html

Open Tuesday to Saturday from 10:00 to 16:00; closed all federal holidays. Free. (Museum location: 21.491130, -158.051331)

Tropic Lightning Museum (above) and Schofield Barrack C Quad (below)

The museum presents over 100 years of Schofield Barracks history focusing upon the 25th Infantry Division with artifacts, photographs and documents that span the period from 1909 to present-day deployment in Iraq. The unit became famous by relieving the Marines at

Guadalcanal in 1942, earning its nickname 'Tropic Lightning.'

The pink, stucco **Schofield Barracks** buildings across Kolekole Avenue are of 1941 vintage. Enter the quad in the center of the buildings to view a scene that may be familiar from several motion pictures about Hawaii and the Pearl Harbor attack. (21.490069, -158.050807)

To access Wheeler Army Airfield: Leave the museum, reverse directions, and go directly through the Visitor's Gate (Lyman Gate) where you will drive over Kunia Road into Wheeler. The gate guards will wave you through; there will be no need to show your identification.

Wheeler Field
Visitors should be processed by Schofield Barracks as described above.

Construction of Wheeler Field upon a former cavalry drill field adjacent to Schofield Barracks started in 1922. By 1941, the field was the main base for fighter (then called pursuit) aircraft in the defense of Oahu and held the 15th and 18th Pursuit Groups flying P-36 Hawk and P-40 Warhawk planes. Today, Wheeler Army Airfield is home to the headquarters of US Army Garrison-Hawaii.

The original 1941 flight line, hangars and barracks survive today. Three information boards mark significant locations in Wheeler Field history. Continue on Wright Ave for 0.3 miles to the large parking area on the right. Walk southwest to Santos Dumont Ave and turn right to an information board describing **Wheeler Field Aviation History** and displaying a bomb scar from 7 December's attack. (21.481712, -158.043945) Walk or drive east on Wright Ave for 0.2 miles to another large parking area where a second information board describes **Wheeler Field on 7 December 1941**. (21.483842, -158.040937) Continue along Wright Ave for 0.3 miles to another large parking area where the third information board describes **Wheeler Field Developmental History**. (21.485305, -158.037150)

Wright Ave and Santos Dumont Ave parallel the runaway which is 0.2 miles to the south. A small display of aircraft can be seen along Santos Dumont Avenue immediately before exiting the field through Kawamura Gate to get back on highway H2. (21.487065, -158.028669)

North Shore
Marconi Wireless Telegraphy Station
56-1095 Kamehameha Highway, Kahuku, Hawaii

The Makai Ranch property is private and access is denied but the buildings can be seen from the end of the public road. (21.706181, -157.973142)

In 1900, Guglielmo Marconi, inventor of telegraphy, was commissioned to establish messaging stations capable of transmitting signals between the Hawaiian Islands. The system was operational on 2 March 1901 and became the first commercial wireless telegraph service in the world. The transoceanic service from the enlarged Kahuku site began service in 1914 as the American Marconi Company (later restructured as the Radio Corporation of America – RCA) and became the most powerful telegraphic station in the world. The US military assumed control of the station during both World Wars. On 10 December 1914, construction commenced for the Kahuku Air Base, which eventually accommodated B-17, B-24, and B-29 bombers. The airfield was abandoned after being severely damaged by a tidal wave in 1946. In 1978 the development of satellite communications ended the useful life of Marconi Kahuku.

The four concrete buildings of the Marconi Wireless Station at Kahuku are on the National Register of Historic Places but lie desolate and abandoned on a level, ocean front parcel at the end of Marconi Drive. The widely separated buildings functioned as the power house / operations building (the largest and most visible), hotel, manager's cottage, and administrative building. The airfield runway has been covered with sand. The remnants present little interest except for specialized historical studies.

Opana Radar Station

Location: Opana Point Station was located at the end of what is now Kawela Camp Road. The site is under military control and access is restricted. (21.685678, -158.009152)

Marconi Station

In 1941, The Signal Corps had six SCR-270 mobile radar sets; each comprised four trucks carrying the transmitter, modulator, water cooler, receiver, oscilloscope, operator, generator and antenna. The antenna tower was truck mounted and unfolded from its transportation position to be a triangular tapering tower rising 45 feet above its base. The other five sites were at Kaena, Ft. Shafter, Koko Head, Haleiwa and Waianae.

Today, a modern Navy telecommunications relay station for the Department of State's Diplomatic Telecommunications Service occupies the top of Opana Hill. Two plaques and an information signboard are along the shore of the Turtle Bay Resort between the pool bar and a row of cottages. (21.70426, -157.99845)

The white domes of the Navy telecommunication equipment may be seen on the horizon to the south.

Ehukai Pillbox Hike (or Sunset Pillbox Hike)

Location: west of Turtle Bay along highway 83.The trailhead is not signed but starts across the parking lot from the Sunset Elementary School. (21.66476, -158.04958)

Opana Radar Memorial

The Ehukai Pillbox trail is better known as the Sunset Pillbox Hike because it offers beautiful views of Ehukai Beach (better known as Banzai Pipeline) and the North Shore coastline. The distance to reach the top of the ridge is short, but can be strenuous, muddy, and poorly marked. The ridge trail leads both east and west; turn left at the junction and head east. The pillboxes on Paumalu Heights were part of Fire Control Station Lena constructed during the war to provide targeting for coastal batteries. The old military bunker is accessible to intrepid explorers. The route is 1.6 miles roundtrip. (Pillbox approximately 21.668417, -158.042799)

Haleiwa Fighter Strip
Location: 0.7 miles north of Haleiwa turn on Kamehameha Highway 83, then turn left onto Kamehameha Place along the north boundary of Haleiwa Beach Park. Proceed to the end of the road. (21.603907, -158.103938)

This obscure former military strip became famous as the only airfield from which American fighters were able to launch a defense against the Pearl Harbor Attack. Originally used as an emergency landing field, in 1941 it had only an unpaved landing strip.

The field was abandoned sometime in the 1960s and is currently overgrown with vegetation although concrete sections of the runway remain visible. The site, now private land, is accessible only after a winding trek through Puaena Point Beach Park.

Haleiwa Beach Park War Memorial
Location: 0.4 miles north of Haleiwa beside Kamehameha Highway 83 at the south end of Haleiwa Beach Park. (21.598057, -158.103269)

The striking white obelisk pays homage to area veterans who died in World War II, the Korean conflict, and the Vietnam War. Of the memorial's sixteen names of soldiers who died in World War II, fourteen were of Japanese ancestry. The park also holds a newly (2016) placed information board describing the pilots and planes that attacked Japanese aircraft from Haleiwa Field.

Dillingham Airfield
Location: 7 miles west of Waialua along Farrington Highway 930 (21.580099, -158.212195)

A communications station called Camp Kawaihapai was established at what is now Dillingham in 1922 along the Oahu Railway and Land Company line on the north shore of Oahu. In the 1920s and 1930s, the railroad transported mobile coast artillery to the site. By 1941, the Army leased additional land and established Mokuleia Airstrip. Curtiss P-40 fighters were deployed at North Shore airstrips at Kahuku, Haleiwa and Mokuleia when the attack on Pearl Harbor took place.

In 1948, the airfield was inactivated and renamed Dillingham Air Force Base in memory of Captain Henry Gaylord Dillingham, a B-29 airman who was killed in action over Kawasaki, Japan on 25 July 1945.

Today, Dillingham is a shared commercial and military airfield that features sky-diving and tourist flights over the islands. Remnants of Second World War defenses remain visible along the airfield perimeter. An abandoned and graffiti scarred **blockhouse** stands along Farrington Road toward the west end of the runway. (21.580899, -158.209520) The western taxiway leads to numerous **abandoned revetments** on the south side of the airfield although they are generally hidden by vegetation. Large plane revetments are at (21.576430, -158.202257) and small plane revetments may be found at (21.576978, -158.195499). The Lockheed L-1011 fuselage stored in this area was used for the television program *Lost*, which was filmed along North Shore beaches.

East Shore
Bellows Field

Bellows Air Force Station is a United States military reservation that now serves as a Marine Corps training area. Tinker Road circles the airfield and provides access to Bellows Field Beach Park. Various sectors of the remaining runways are used by the 298th Regiment of the Hawaiian Army National Guard. The 18th Force Support Squadron presently operates Bellows Air Force Station. Both are therefore restricted. Original runway locations are at (21.357774, -157.715253) but are not accessible.

A brass plaque mounted upon a stone platform and fieldstone plinth near the entrance gate to Bellows Air Force Station commemorates the sacrifice of members of the **15th Marine Expeditionary Unit** whose MV-22 Osprey tilt rotor aircraft crashed on a training mission on 17 May 2015. Two Marines were killed and twenty-two others injured. (21.3634, -157.7106)

Naval Air Station Kaneohe Bay (now Marine Corps Base Hawaii)
Location: The main gate is at the far northeast end of highway H3. Access is restricted to those with military ID. (21.436423, -157.756705)

Although decommissioned in 1949, three years later the Marine Corps re-commissioned the idle airfield as Marine Corps Air Station Kaneohe Bay.

The **Pacific War Memorial in Hawaii** is located immediately inside the main gate. The bronze image of the raising of the United States flag on 23 February 1945 on Mount Suribachi, Iwo Jima signifies Allied determination, jointness of effort, and victory with great sacrifice in the Pacific. The statue is a duplicate of the National Iwo Jima Memorial in Newington, Connecticut and varies slightly from the version prominent in Arlington, Virginia. The location is significant since the Marines trained for the Iwo Jima mission on Oahu, Maui, and Guam. The poignant cluster of men struggling to raise the flag is mounted upon ten polished granite panels that form the base of the monument. Inscribed across the top is Admiral Chester W. Nimitz's famous quote, '...Among the Americans who served on Iwo Island, uncommon valor was a common virtue.' Inscriptions on the reverse side of the monument recognize the contributions of the 3rd, 4th, and 5th Marine Divisions during the battle. End panels feature an Iwo Jima map depicting the plan of the attack and the civilian support provided by Hawaii residents for those who trained and regrouped in Hawaii between the Pacific battles. (21.436249, -157.757370)

Lanikai Pillbox Hike Trail (also known as the Kaiwa Ridge Trail)
Trailhead: signed at short unnamed street off Kaelepulu Drive near the Mid-Pacific Country Club. (21.3903, -157.71943) Parking is a problem on local streets; public parking is available at Kailua Beach.
Pillbox locations: (21.387296, -157.717538) and (21.385614, -157.716579)

This popular hiking trail strenuously ascends the Kaiwa Ridge and follows the peak for 1.3 miles, one way, offering spectacular views of the east coast of Oahu including the Mokulua Islands and Kailua and Lanikai Beaches. Farther distant are Kaneohe Bay, Chinaman's Hat, Waimanalo Bay, and the Makapu'u Lighthouse. The two graffiti-covered observation pillboxes are nothing special, but they provide destination points for the trail. One pillbox can be seen from residential Aalapapa Drive.

West Shore
Ewa Marine Corps Air Station (MCAS)

Ewa was declared excess and disestablished in 1952. The airfield's property was absorbed into Naval Air Station (NAS) - Barbers Point and parts of Ewa were incorporated into the Barbers Point Golf Course.

A stone platform bearing a black granite plaque at the Navy's Barbers Point Golf Course near the clubhouse commemorates the four Marines who lost their lives on 7 December.[67] An adjacent informational sign identifies the runway location for MCAS Ewa and describes the Japanese attack incorporating graphic images of the resulting damage. (21.32475, -158.03923)

West Side Pillbox Trail

Location: unsigned trailhead on of south side of Kaukama Road 0.3 mile east of Farrington Highway. (21.40458, -158.17241; pillbox locations: 21.400967, -158.170591)

The ridge above Farrington Highway holds a cluster of five pillboxes at Puu O Hulu that formed a **Fire Control Station**. In recent years the structures became graffiti marred. Local authorities covered the 'artwork' by painting some, but not all,of the exteriors bright pink. The trail quickly and strenuously ascends the ridge and then follows the crest to the pillboxes locations whose major features are the views to the west. They are visible from the highway silhouetted against

West Side pink pillbox

the sky, but the high-speed and lack of a shoulder precluded safe viewing; although a short driveway to the Oahu Civil Defense station (21.401409, -158.175251) offers a safe turn off.

---

67   They are Sergeant William E Latschau Jr, Private William G Turner (recipient of a Bronze Star), Pfc Edward S Lawrence, and Sergeant Carlo A Michaletto.